Chemical Dependency
and the African American

Chemical Dependency and the African American

SECOND EDITION

Peter Bell

Hazelden
Center City, Minnesota 55012-0176

1-800-328-0094
1-651-213-4590 (Fax)
www.hazelden.org

ISBN 1-56838-881-0

06 05 04   6 5 4 3 2

Cover design by David Spohn
Interior design by David Spohn
Typesetting by Tursso Companies

Contents

Illustrations

Figures

Acknowledgments

I want to acknowledge my wife, Sharon, and my children, Jessica and Brian, for all their love and support. I also want to thank Krystn Rice, my administrative assistant, and Rebecca Post, my editor, for their assistance with this publication.

Finally, I want to thank my parents, Earl and Merle Bell, my sister, Merle, and my grandmother Sidonia Black for their guidance and support. It is through the foundation they provided me that I was able to enter into recovery twenty-eight years ago. Throughout my life, my family has challenged me to speak what in my heart I believe to be true. This book is written in that spirit.

Introduction

A major dilemma that has long faced the chemical dependency field is how to recognize legitimate differences in clients without allowing those differences to be used as excuses. Historically, the field of chemical dependency has simply denied or minimized differences. This denial has coexisted with the rapid development of programs targeting a wide array of "special populations" defined by age, gender, race, class, sexual orientation, or religious affiliation.

In essence, the question is not "Does race or culture matter?" but "How should the issues, feelings, or life experiences of race or culture be reflected in our prevention and treatment programs?" The field can no longer say it is treating the whole person while ignoring important feelings and issues that result from being the one among the many. This concern must be balanced, however, with the fact that many individuals will use their race, culture, or class as a way to protect or rationalize their alcohol and other drug use. The best way to illustrate this idea is with the chart on page 2.

Many white counselors rightfully fear, for example, that African American and other minority clients will practice a cultural one-upmanship of "racial authority" by stating flatly that whites cannot relate to them or help them due to a lack of understanding and sensitivity. In truth, as members of the human family, all racial and ethnic groups have more that unites than divides. All cultures have common values of family, friends, health, and education. All value productivity and the desire to create healthy communities. Our

The Cultural Counseling Balance

Clients Using Differences as Excuses

Acknowledging and Accepting Differences
While Not Allowing Them to Be Used as Excuses

Counselors Ignoring or Minimizing Legitimate Differences

©2002 by Hazelden Foundation   Figure 1

core values and goals are often amazingly similar.

However, culture does impact how these values are prioritized and expressed. For instance, Native Americans will express family and religious values differently than people of German descent. Equally important are the feelings and responses that result from the interaction between cultural groups. If one cultural group practices a type of chauvinism—believing that one worldview is the only acceptable one—misunderstanding, conflict, and significant emotional pain will result.

There is a cliché in counseling circles: "You cannot facilitate growth past your own." Counselors cannot help a client look at or resolve an issue with which the counselor is unfamiliar. The treatment field has largely rejected this notion and taken the following position: *feelings* = *empathy*. This formula suggests that one individual's hurt or anger feels the same as another individual's. While there may be a measure of truth to this idea, it is somewhat limited. A more complete equation is *feelings + experiences = empathy.*

In order to truly empathize with an individual, a counselor needs to have some appreciation for the experiences that caused a particular feeling. The best illustration of a common mistake is a counselor telling a client who has lost a child, "I know how you feel"—when, in fact, the counselor has not had a similar experience. Empathy is, however, only one component of a successful counseling relationship. The skill, training, and experience of the therapist are of greater importance in the overall clinical relationship than the unique experiences of the therapist and client.

CHAPTER 1

Theories of Addiction and Their Cultural Relevance

There is little serious debate on the question of whether culture affects alcohol and other drug abuse. The real questions are *how* and *to what extent* there is an impact.

Three major factors appear to determine whether an individual becomes chemically dependent:

1. the addictive potential of the chemical of choice (for example, crack cocaine versus marijuana)
2. environmental conditions (for example, poverty, educational level, employment, family structure)
3. genetic predisposition to alcohol and other drug abuse (family history of addiction)

An individual's chemical dependency can result from either the overwhelming presence of one of these three factors or, most likely, with two or three of these factors working in tandem. The following three examples illustrate this point:

1. Some individuals come from supportive families with no family history of addiction, experience no significant peer pressure, and are well educated, employed, and well adjusted emotionally.

Nevertheless, when these individuals use a highly addictive substance, such as crack or heroin, they run a high risk of becoming dependent on the drug. The addictive potential of the chemical is the key factor in their addiction.

2. Other individuals come from neighborhoods filled with drugs, have few emotional coping skills, and have significant peer pressure to use drugs. These individuals may have no family history of addiction, yet when they use marijuana or other drugs that have a lower addictive potential, they may become dependent.

3. A third group of individuals comes from an environment where they have limited exposure to drugs, experience little peer pressure to use drugs, and have adequate emotional coping skills. But these individuals have a genetic predisposition for addiction. They can become quickly addicted to whatever chemical they use.

The addictive potential of a particular chemical is, for the most part, outside cultural considerations, though the culture can certainly affect the pace at which the addiction progresses.

Environmental factors contribute to addiction. Theoretically, changing individuals' environments—improving schools, increasing employment options, establishing clear community values and rules regarding alcohol and other drug use, controlling how alcohol is marketed, and deglamorizing the drug and crime lifestyle—would help with both prevention and treatment activities.

Of course, the environmental factor that most influences an individual's chemical use is the family. Society has had, at best, mixed results on exerting positive, long-term change on multiproblem dysfunctional families.

Genetic predisposition to addiction is a subject closely scrutinized by African Americans and other minority groups because many fear that genetic predisposition will increase stereotyping and bias. This may, in turn, open the door to the concept of *rational discrimination*, the notion that certain types of stereotypes are logical, rational, and based on applying statistical probability to a situation. If, for example, 30 to 50 percent of Native Americans have an alcohol abuse problem and it is proven that genetics played a role, would not landlords, employers, or health insurance companies be tempted to discriminate in their rental, hiring, or insuring activities? Further, this action would be seen as a rational behavior rather than one that reflects racial bias.

TWO THEORIES OF ADDICTION

Currently, alcohol and other drug abuse treatment services generally subscribe to one of two theories on addiction: the disease model or the environmental-secondary model.

Disease Model

Dr. E. M. Jellinek was one of the first to popularize the disease model of addiction in the 1940s through the 1960s. His Jellinek Chart is still widely used in treatment centers today.

My definition of the disease model follows:

> Chemical dependency is a biomedical and psychosocial illness. It has a genetic base that is significantly influenced by environmental factors, which include the addictive potential of the chemical being abused. It is a primary, progressive, pathological, and love-trust relationship with a mood-altering chemical.
>
> Chemical dependency also results in behavior that is in repeated conflict with personal values and goals. The individual's ability to function physically or

mentally in a competent manner is often impaired.

Chemical dependency can be most successfully prevented, diagnosed, and treated when the cultural context in which the chemical use or abuse developed is taken into account.

Three components of this definition have cultural relevancy:

- Addiction is primary.
- Addiction is progressive.
- Addiction is a feeling disease.

Addiction is primary

This simply means that an existing alcohol and drug problem must be addressed before any other coexisting problem. Vernon Johnson, founder of the Johnson Institute, used to make a fist with his left hand and cover it with his right hand. The fingers on his left hand represented the many problems associated with alcohol and drug abuse, such as divorce, unemployment, crime, bankruptcy, and depression. These problems, however, cannot be effectively addressed until the alcohol and drug abuse covering them (represented by the right hand) are removed.

The African American community has always had problems accepting this concept. One reason is that many African American leaders firmly believe that racism and oppression are the causes of many, if not all, of the problems that affect their communities. In addition, African Americans' personal, legal, or financial problems often will have predated their addiction, giving credence to the notion that all they have to do is address the underlying "causes" of addiction in order to overcome it.

Addiction is progressive

This concept states that addicts and alcoholics will experience continued deterioration of their lives until, and unless, they address the primary problem of addiction and abstain from the use of all mood-altering chemicals. Some proponents of the disease model even believe that the disease progresses when an individual is clean and sober. The following chart illustrates how addiction is progressive.

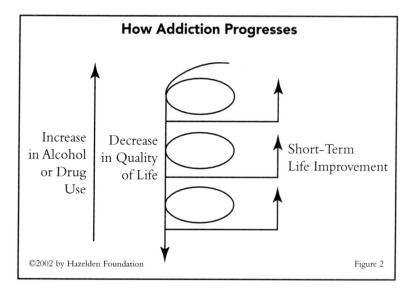

How Addiction Progresses

Increase in Alcohol or Drug Use

Decrease in Quality of Life

Short-Term Life Improvement

©2002 by Hazelden Foundation

Figure 2

As this chart illustrates, the life of an alcohol or drug abuser tends to deteriorate as his or her "using career" progresses.

There are brief periods of improvement (illustrated by the upward arrows), usually brought on by a crisis in the individual's life. He or she may be threatened with divorce, loss of a job, or significant embarrassment. When this happens, the addict may stop using for a brief period of time. These upward spurts in an addict's life are what cause family members and friends to feel confused often about how to approach the problem. In fact, family members sometimes figure out how to get their needs met even while the individual is actively using alcohol or other drugs.

Many young people raised with chemically dependent family members experience uneven development that results from parents putting their wants and needs first. Young people may be required to assist with activities usually reserved for adults: caring for younger siblings, maintaining the household, shopping for groceries, or even helping to pay the rent. This situation is made more complicated if the chemically dependent person is in and out of recovery. When this is the case, the oldest child is often moved back and forth from a child to a parent role, causing a great deal of confusion and resentment in the process. This role displacement and uneven adolescent development is the core basis of both codependency and COA (child of an alcoholic) issues.

When there is only one parent in the household, and he or she is chemically dependent, the situation becomes even more difficult. Then, the oldest child takes on a parent role and must protect the other siblings from the physical or emotional abuse of the parent. This requires the child to grow up, often before he or she is emotionally ready. Emotional scars created in such a situation are often deep and lifelong.

As mentioned earlier, many believe that the illness continues to progress even during periods of abstinence. Whether this is true or not, it is clear that each relapse causes the downward spiral to accelerate. For example, it can take an individual twenty years of drinking and drug use to go from the top of the spiral to the bottom. But if this person enters a sober period, then relapses, the downward spiral may take only two or three years. A third relapse could result in a bottoming-out time of two or three weeks. As the disease progresses, the coil gets tighter and tighter. The periods of time when things improve are also of a shorter duration.

Family members will often recommend actions associated with the upward swings of the spiral. This may include marriage counseling, a return to school, or attempts to control chemical use. An example is when a spouse will say, "I will quit drinking hard liquor and just have a beer or two on the weekend" or, "I'll lay off the crack pipe and just smoke a little weed every now and then."

The downward spiral of addiction looks exactly the same for all racial and ethnic groups, with a couple of key exceptions.

First, many individuals of color have a higher tolerance of *emotional pain*. This reality allows minorities to survive in an inhospitable world that often only conditionally accepts them. In that context, tolerance of emotional pain can be a useful tool of cultural survival and adaptation. It is not uncommon in communities of color to hear stories of surviving and even thriving in very harsh conditions. This, in effect, can become a rite of passage. Unfortunately, it can also cause individuals of color and their families to accept, tolerate, and even normalize unacceptable and inappropriate behavior. The result is that problems of all sorts, including alcohol and drug abuse, domestic violence, and crime, often progress to a severe stage before they are recognized and addressed. Most troubling, dysfunctional behavior can become normalized, accepted, and even celebrated by a cultural group.

Second, most individuals from any racial or ethnic group learn about addiction from a family member or friend who received treatment. Health care in the United States is largely a word-of-mouth industry. We often find a doctor, dentist, or therapist from a neighbor, friend, or family member. It stands to reason that the treatment experience of an individual we love and trust will significantly influence our views. Communities are also affected by this dynamic. If the treatment experience of many individuals was successful, the view of and openness to treatment in the community is enhanced. If unsuccessful, the opposite is the case.

Complicating the situation, African Americans who are successful in treatment often are given the message that in order to maintain a clean-and-sober lifestyle they must leave the African American community. Those who fail often return to the community. The destructive impact of individuals who failed in treatment on family and friends' receptivity to treatment cannot be overstated.

The fact that African American individuals get into treatment later in the progression of the disease is also significant:

- Later entry into treatment often means entering via the court system, as opposed to self-referral or intervention by family members or employers.
- Later entry lowers the probability for successful treatment and long-term recovery. The alcoholic or addict who comes to treatment late in the progression of the disease is less likely to have an intact, supportive family or a job, both of which are important predictors of recovery success.
- Later entry is costly because inpatient treatment, long-term treatment, or both are usually required.
- Later entry increases the likelihood that the alcoholic or addict will have contracted diseases, such as HIV or hepatitis, or will have exprienced other physical limitations resulting from accidents and so on, which are often caused by chemical dependency.

In addition, individuals who enter treatment later in the progression of the illness are more likely to need *habilitation* rather than *rehabilitation*. Rehabilitation assumes the existence of positive values and goals that the client has strayed from and needs to return to. The goal of counseling is often to help clients reconnect to those forgotten norms. For some, rehabilitation is a misguided effort because they never held positive goals and values. These are the individuals who have never held a job or been in a healthy relationship. They may be illiterate and committed to a deviant criminal lifestyle. These clients require habilitation: the development of positive norms and values. This is a much more difficult task.

Our entire chemical dependency treatment system is built on the assumption of rehabilitation, not habilitation. Clients now come to treatment either very early in their chemical abuse or else very, very late. The effects of this reality have the potential to affect the entire chemical dependency treatment system in this country.

Addiction is a feeling disease

Addiction is a vicious cycle. A chemical is used to medicate an uncomfortable or unwelcome feeling, but the use of the chemical also escalates the very feelings the person seeks to avoid. In the short term, the chemical provides relief for one's troubles. In the long term, the chemical makes one's problems worse. What bad marriage, shaky financial situation, or bout of depression is not aggravated by alcohol or other drug abuse? The feelings—hurt, loneliness, shame, anger, guilt—that accompany these situations are temporarily medicated but ultimately increased by chemical use.

What is often not recognized is the significant role that culture plays in our emotional life. Culture often establishes the context for our feelings, telling us which are okay, which should be avoided, and how each should be expressed. For example, different messages are given to men and women regarding the legitimacy of anger and hurt, how these feelings should be expressed, and what role each should play. Simply stated, men in our culture have more permission to recognize, experience, and even act on their anger than do women. The opposite is true for hurt.

The disease model has much evidence to support it. It is, in fact, the basis of this book. Other theories of addiction, such as the environmental-secondary model, appear to be gaining ground among racial minorities. Until the practitioners who adhere to the disease model recognize the significance of cultural issues, it is likely that attempts to find an alternative will continue.

Environmental-Secondary Model

Although less formally postulated than the disease model, and more often discussed verbally rather than seen in print, the environmental-secondary model appears to have greater support among minorities than among the white community. This model is more responsive to cultural issues. The main distinction between the two models relates to the cause of addiction, which is relatively unimportant in treatment based on the disease model. Adherents to the disease model may agree that the environment could be a causal factor in addiction, but they would not necessarily change the method of treatment. A counselor using the disease model would commonly tell a client, "Don't be concerned with why you became an addict or an alcoholic. Only be concerned with your recovery from addiction."

Many professionals who work in related fields, such as mental health, housing, welfare, and job training, adhere to the environmental-secondary model of addiction. They often regard underlying issues of family instability, crime, and unemployment as primary and regard addiction as secondary. Their approach to therapy often addresses these underlying issues. If these issues can be resolved, according to those who support this theory, the addict or alcoholic will be cured and can return to social drinking or other drug use.

Proponents of the environmental-secondary theory do not subscribe to the principle of cross-addiction; they believe, for example, that a cocaine addict may be able to drink responsibly. This theory of addiction got its start in therapeutic communities in the early 1960s and lives on today in the harm-reduction movement, which focuses on reducing the harmful effects of alcohol and drug addiction rather than on addressing the addiction itself. This approach has gained great popularity in Europe.

Criticism of the Disease Model

Historically, the disease model has received more acceptance from the white community than from the African American community. While there are both supporters and critics of the disease model in the African American community, there is far less consensus that the disease model is the best model of care. Many minorities have concerns that followers of the disease model resist acknowledging or addressing issues of cultural difference.

References to or discussions about cultural issues by clients can be viewed by disease-model counselors as excuses or cop-outs. Some counselors seem to fear that acknowledging cultural differences will negatively empower clients, who will then reject the rest of the treatment program as not relevant to their lives.

When an African American or other minority client raises an issue relating to culture, that individual may be dismissed with one of the following clichés:

- "We are here to talk about our disease."
- "Chemical dependency is a democratic illness affecting all groups of individuals."
- "Stop trying to be unique."
- "We all have the same feelings."
- "We all have the same illness."
- "I will treat everyone the same."
- "You are just using race as an excuse to avoid treatment or to continue using drugs."

It is often hard for a counselor to determine when a client is using his or her culture as a shield and when he or she has a legitimate cultural explanation for a behavior, particularly because denial and manipulation are so prevalent in all chemically dependent individuals.

Criticism of the Environmental-Secondary Model

As stated earlier, the African American community is somewhat resistant to the idea that addiction is primary. It often views alcohol and other drug abuse as growing out of racism, poverty, or lack of opportunity. While strong institutional, economic, and cultural roadblocks can impede recovery, it is hard to imagine an individual or cultural group making significant progress in addressing alcohol and other drug abuse while viewing it only as a secondary problem.

While racism has had a devastating effect on every aspect of life in African American communities, it is difficult to make a strong factual case for racism as the *major* cause of addiction among individuals of color. If racism and oppression were the major factors in producing addiction, there would have been much more alcohol and other drug abuse among African Americans fifty to seventy-five years ago, when racism was more virulent than it is today.

In addition, there is no clear indication that oppressed groups worldwide have higher rates of alcohol and drug abuse. In fact, some cultural and religious groups who have experienced oppression have had lower rates of substance abuse. The Jewish community is perhaps the best example.

METHADONE TREATMENT PROGRAMS

The environmental-secondary model of addiction can result in a nonabstinence approach. An example is the use of methadone, which is the primary method of treatment for heroin addicts in the United States. This approach is used widely in minority communities.

Methadone, when used for a short detoxification period, can be consistent with the disease model of addiction. But when methadone is used for *maintenance* and *treatment* during an extended period of time, it becomes a bridge to cross-addiction, as heroin addicts have a high propensity for abusing other substances. Some of the critical questions that need to be asked in the African American community about methadone maintenance are the following:

- Is it appropriate for government to underwrite its citizens' addiction to any drug, particularly when the overdose death rate for methadone in some areas is higher than that of heroin?
- Are clients using and abusing alcohol and other drugs while on methadone?
- Does the existence of methadone serve as an incentive for addicts to start using heroin again, because they know there is a relatively painless way to "come off" their habit? In other words, does the withdrawal experience have a deterrent effect on an addict who considers using again?
- Does the existence of methadone create a disincentive for clients to try a drug-free approach? Does methadone in effect lower expectations for client outcome?

Methadone is strongly supported by the harm-reduction movement because it is a form of social control and has the potential to lower crime. Methadone-dependent individuals are also less likely to share needles, which in turn helps decrease the spread of HIV and hepatitis. For many policy makers, the most attractive aspect of methadone maintenance programs is the fact that they are relatively inexpensive compared to other forms of treatment.

The primary issue, however, is the long-term effectiveness of methadone maintenance programs in changing and improving individuals' lives. There are strong feelings among some African Americans that methadone should not be used as primary treatment. One suggestion is that all potential methadone clients demonstrate, at a minimum, two failures in drug-free programs before being admitted to a methadone program. In addition, those clients must clearly demonstrate their current addiction to heroin. Another consideration would be to eliminate the practice of methadone maintenance in favor of rapid (fourteen to twenty-one days) methadone-assisted detoxification.

THE CHALLENGE FOR COUNSELORS

While there is room in the disease model to accommodate cultural differences, many chemical dependency treatment professionals are only now becoming aware of the critical significance culture plays among racial groups in recovery.

The premise of this book is as follows:

> Treatment based on the disease model needs to develop a mechanism for chemically dependent individuals to talk about racial identity issues and cultural differences, without allowing those differences to be used as excuses to avoid treatment or deep-seated emotional issues.

If counselors and other staff in chemical dependency agencies are unfamiliar or uncomfortable with cultural issues, these issues can then be used as a cop-out by clients to avoid treatment. The answer to this dilemma lies in education and understanding. Counselors who understand cultural issues can then deal with them, rather than deny them out of a lack of familiarity or ability to address them. Counselors can then objectively address cultural issues and determine whether they are real or a form of cultural manipulation.

CHAPTER 2

Impact of Alcohol and Drug Abuse on the African American Community

The fact that the African American community has significant challenges is beyond serious debate. Virtually every problem from housing, health, education, crime, and employment is more severe in African American communities. Debate rages on the causes of and solutions to this tragic situation.

Without question, these problems exist in a cultural and political context, significantly influencing each other. Problems with education lead to underemployment and crime that, in turn, affect housing. What often goes unexplored is the significant role alcohol and other drugs plays in both causing and exacerbating these concerns. It is a chicken-and-egg question whether alcohol and drug abuse causes much of the poverty, undereducation, and health issues in the African American community or whether it is the result.

What is clear is that these problems cannot be successfully resolved in the midst of significant alcohol and drug abuse. There is little to gain, for example, in trying to help a drug-dependent person get a job before treating the drug abuse. Alcohol and drug addiction needs to be treated as a primary problem—when someone is addicted, little lasting progress can be made in improving other conditions.

A special challenge exists in trying to treat alcohol and drug problems in multiproblem minority communities. As stated earlier, most chemical dependency treatment is based on the concept of rehabilitation: returning the individual to former positive values and reconnecting him or her to discarded goals. The challenge with people who have low incomes and many problems is that they may never have learned positive social values. When an individual grows up believing that education is silly and that a straight job is for chumps, while at the same time loving the drama of crime, habilitation not rehabilitation is necessary.

These individuals often enter treatment under court order. They often provide a particular challenge for treatment professionals who do not understand or relate to the lifestyle and values of this group.

Alcohol and drug abuse in African American communities is intertwined with six major concerns: health care, crime, family stability, employment and income, education, and housing.

HEALTH CARE

Life expectancy for African Americans continues to be significantly lower than for whites. In 1999, the life expectancy for African Americans was 5.9 years less than that of whites, according to the Centers for Disease Control and Prevention. While the difference has been narrowing during the past twenty years, it is still a significant health care concern.[1]

In 1999, the drug-induced mortality rate was 1.4 times higher for African Americans than for whites. The alcohol-induced mortality rate was also 1.4 times higher.[2] Both of these figures exclude death from accidents and homicides, which are closely linked to alcohol and drug abuse and are also more frequent in African American populations.

The service implication of these health care issues is clear. Increased efforts should be made to help health care professionals working in African American communities to diagnose and intervene earlier in the progression of alcohol and drug addiction. Where possible, inner-city health care clinics and emergency rooms would benefit from having staff members with chemical dependency expertise.

CRIME

While many view the war on drugs as a war on black America, virtually everyone agrees that crime is unacceptably high in African American communities and disproportionately victimizes those communities.

While African Americans make up 12 percent of the overall U.S. population, they comprise 46.3 percent of individuals who are incarcerated in federal and state institutions, according to the Bureau of Justice Statistics.[3] In addition, 9.7 percent of black males between the ages of twenty-five and twenty-nine are in prison, compared to 1.1 percent of white males.[4]

Crime has a significant impact on housing, economic development, and community stability. The role of drugs and crime is twofold: dealing in drugs has become a form of employment, and committing crime is used as a method to support a drug habit. Many African American youths become involved in criminal activity that can include selling drugs (often to whites) before they become addicted. In addition to the money and status this activity provides, crime has evolved into a rite of passage for segments of the African American community.

In white America, by contrast, criminal activity is not associated with drugs until far into the progression of addiction. The gateway process for whites typically starts with cigarette smoking and alcohol use and progresses to other drugs and eventually to crime. In most instances, white individuals who are caught selling drugs are addicted to them and get referred to a treatment program.

Another challenge in the African American community is denial by families with alcohol and drug problems. African American parents, like their white counterparts, often deny or downplay their children's involvement with drugs. The motivation to deny is heightened when children contribute to family finances or, at a minimum, are not taking resources away from the family. When parents know little about drug treatment programs and see examples of treatment failures, they tend to tolerate their children's dysfunctional behavior for a longer period of time.

In white communities, intervention is often brought on by economic problems associated with drug abuse. In black communities, a family's finances can actually improve in the short-term as a result of a family member's involvement with chemicals. This creates another barrier to treatment.

African American youths addicted to a criminal lifestyle as well as to drugs are likely to need habilitative, culturally specific treatment rather than rehabilitative programs. These services need to focus on basic education and job readiness. If the current trend continues toward outpatient treatment, habilitative treatment programs may not be developed because they often need to be inpatient and longer term.

FAMILY STABILITY

The decline in family stability in the African American community is a significant concern. While the number of single-parent households has dropped recently, it is still relatively high. In 2000, 68.7 percent of births to unmarried mothers were to non-Hispanic blacks.[5] This reality, coupled with a high divorce rate, means that the majority of African American children will not live in two-parent households.

Teen Pregnancy

Teen pregnancy is one of the links in the chain of family breakdown. While the fertility rate of African American teenagers has declined significantly in recent years, it is more than double the rate for white teenagers.[6]

Abuse

Child abuse in African American families may be partly attributable to a cultural belief that spanking children is necessary in childrearing—a belief that is increasingly challenged by the broader community. In other words, within segments of the African American community, spanking a child is not seen as abusive. It is seen as a traditional and legitimate method of discipline.

The rate of violence against spouses is 35 percent higher for African American families than for white families, according to the National Crime Victimization Survey.[7]

Family Income Drained by Drug Use

Young, undereducated, poor, single African American women who have children may be particularly susceptible to using drugs for a variety of reasons:

- the responsibility of rearing children by themselves without financial or parenting assistance from a partner
- the feelings of hopelessness that their lives will not improve in the foreseeable future
- the availability of drugs in most low-income housing projects and inner-city neighborhoods
- the pressure to use chemicals by friends and family members

When poor, single parents begin using drugs, their lives quickly unravel. These parents are often resource poor in terms of education, parenting skills, coping skills, and any assistance from a partner in raising the children.

Drug abuse depletes both emotional and financial resources. People living on the financial edge have a smaller margin for error. Poor people—who are disproportionately victims of theft and robbery—are generally far more devastated than middle-class people who are victims of theft. Poor people usually have fewer resources, in the form of insurance or savings, to help them through crises.

Family instability is a reality that accompanies the lives of addicts and alcoholics and wreaks havoc on their children. For individuals in these situations, treatment programs must focus on habilitation rather than rehabilitation. Culturally sensitive approaches are needed that focus on instilling positive values. In addition, treatment programs that work with low income, inner-city communities should focus on parenting issues.

EMPLOYMENT AND INCOME

Poverty and unemployment continue to be major issues in the African American community. The poverty rate is 29 percent for African Americans, compared to 10 percent for whites.[8] The median income for African Americans is $18,000, compared to $33,000 for whites.[9]

Any meaningful effort to improve the employment of African Americans must address the alcohol and drug problems of the unemployed and underemployed. African Americans are not only less likely to be hired but also more likely to be disciplined or fired. In addition to issues of discrimination, some of these employment-related problems stem from alcohol and drug abuse.

A major creative step that can be taken in this area is the development of client assistance programs (CAPs). These programs could be placed in various human, social, and vocational rehabilitative programs that service inner-city communities. They are similar to traditional employee assistance and student assistance programs, providing assessment and intervention services for individuals who are interested in turning their lives around.

Traditional employee assistance programs (EAPs) would positively affect industries that hire large numbers of low-income individuals, particularly the fast-food industry. Employee assistance programs have generally proved to be cost effective in industry, and there is no reason to believe they would be any less cost effective in industries that pay minimum-wage salaries. EAPs would likely cause a modest reduction in the job turnover rate that would justify the cost of creating these new EAPs. Tax incentives could also be used to encourage companies to develop these programs.

EDUCATION

The African American community has made significant gains regarding education. However, it is still far behind the white community in important areas, such as high school and college completion. In addition, African Americans lag behind their white counterparts in test scores. For example, 11.4 percent of African Americans have a bachelor's degree, compared to 18.6 percent of whites. More than 21 percent of African Americans have not finished high school, compared to 11 percent of whites.[10] Further, truancy, discipline, parental involvement with students, and the competency of teachers, especially in inner-city schools, remain important issues.

The role of drugs in hampering education is a widely discussed topic in society today. Drug use appears to correlate with truancy, attention deficit disorder (ADD), behavioral problems, and poor academic performance. Drug use is obviously prohibited in schools. Yet, many inner-city classrooms lack sufficient staff and mechanisms to enforce these policies vigorously. Drug use in the schools appears to have a twofold effect: the person using is not learning and is often disruptive, which affects the learning opportunities of others.

Student assistance programs need to emphasize services to children whose parents are addicts and alcoholics. These children are at high risk of becoming addicted themselves. School-based services also need to address the marginal episodic abuser, the individual who uses but who does not require treatment.

While implementing drug-prevention curricula, educators should recognize that youths who are at the highest risk for drug abuse often have difficulty learning by traditional methods. As a result, prevention efforts should be reconfigured for experiential or kinesthetic learners.

HOUSING

Home ownership is clearly a major building block to stable communities. Home ownership is associated with lower crime rates and better school achievement, resulting from stable attendance patterns. Owning a home is also the number one way that Americans build wealth, which can be used to fund college education or provide financial support in retirement.

The picture of home ownership in African American communities is mixed. While the rate of ownership is growing faster in black America than white America, it is still at 47.1 percent for African Americans and 73.6 percent for whites.[11] There are many reasons for this situation, including racial bias in the sale and financing of housing.

Alcohol and drug abuse also plays a significant and often hidden role in two key areas: credit problems and low housing appreciation. Credit problems are perhaps the single biggest factor preventing African Americans from purchasing homes. While statistics are hard to find, credit counselors quickly identify unresolved alcohol and drug abuse as a major factor in bad credit.

The effects of housing appreciation are more subtle. African Americans tend to live in communities where housing appreciation is the lowest. This has a significant impact on the wealth-building aspect of housing and is directly related to the impact that crime and drugs have on a community.

In summary, not one of these significant issues—health care, crime, family stability, employment and income, education, or housing—can be seriously addressed without acknowledging the complexities of drug and alcohol abuse in African American communities.

CHAPTER 3

Racial Identity Adjustment Issues

An article of faith in human services has been that counselors from a particular racial or ethnic group have always been more effective when "working with their own." This idea, while on its face makes sense, is overly simplistic. It presupposes that racial and ethnic groups are homogeneous, which, of course, is not true. Hypothetically, who would be the best counselor for Tiger Woods, the famous golfer? A counselor from a Thai or African American background, or perhaps someone with similar wealth and fame? Who would work best with a client from a Hispanic culture when that client is genetically black, or the Korean child who was adopted at birth by white parents?

For most of us, race and culture are just two factors that influence our identity. Other factors of gender, class, religion, geography, and nationality influence our ideas, feelings, and emotional state. For many African American clients, an African American counselor is preferable. For other African American clients, issues of gender or class may be more important. In fact, these preferences could change depending on the issue a client is addressing.

As a result, treatment centers need more than an affirmative action strategy to address these issues. Treatment programs along with mental health counseling centers and counseling training programs need to teach all counselors to identify and address a wide range of cultural adjustment issues.

Cultural adaptation, for the vast majority of minority individuals, happens in adolescence. Our parents, relatives, teachers, and religious institutions help define us in a gender, class, and cultural context. They help establish rules for individual behavior patterns, and they set expectations. However, when society is changing rapidly, when we move to a new neighborhood or country, or when our parents are of different races, the signals we get can be confusing or contradictory and cause a great deal of emotional stress. In addition, each culture sends strong messages and stereotypes about different racial or ethnic groups. What is a young African American boy who is a poor athlete to think of himself when constantly confronted with the athletic prowess of high-profile black athletes who receive extensive media coverage? What self-image will an African American girl with strong African features have in a society that has an unrelenting white standard of beauty that is celebrated by the media at every turn? What feelings might the exceptionally bright African American student have when white peers and teachers view him as the "special one"?

These issues, like many others, are often resolved in adolescence. However, chemical use and abuse can and often does limit or retard their successful resolution. When these issues surface in treatment, a conspiracy of silence often develops between the counselor (if of another race or culture) and the client around these unresolved cultural adjustment issues. The client tends to deny or minimize the existence of these painful issues that are often buried under significant amounts of emotional scar tissue.

Counselors often feel very inadequate in addressing these issues. They often feel cumbersome and unsure of the best approaches. Compare it to throwing a baseball with your opposite hand or attempting to provide counseling services in a foreign language. It's as if addressing these issues intrudes on a very personal family issue where the rules are not at all clear. In addition, most counselors don't want to appear culturally ignorant or insensitive and often are concerned about charges of racism. A further complication is the amount of "racial fatigue" in this country. People are just plain tired of and overwhelmed by race problems that appear to have no clear-cut solutions. When issues of race or culture are raised in virtually any context, one can sense the response from all racial groups of "Oh, boy, here we go again." In many cases, the easiest path for both client and counselor is simply silence and denial.

In truth, we have not found the language to deal with race in the United States. We often paint these issues in stark black–and–white terms with little or no nuance of gray.

Racial issues are about much more than slavery, discrimination, affirmative action, poverty, police brutality, crime, or poorly planned pregnancies. The key issues can no longer be boiled down to who is guilty and who is innocent. The most important issues are often connected to feelings we have about what it means to be loyal and authentic. Other issues include responding to stereotypes, dealing with a limited standard of beauty, and struggling to survive in two different worlds with conflicting sets of expectations.

COLOR CONSCIOUSNESS

One major emotional gap between African Americans and whites is the existence, or lack, of *color consciousness*. If you ask a white person and a black person to identify and prioritize major personal traits, race would likely be prioritized differently by each. Many whites simply don't view themselves as white. African Americans, on the other hand, have a high degree of racial awareness and see their race as a central organizational principle in their lives.

This gap regarding both the existence and importance of race in self-image creates a great deal of confusion and misunderstanding between individuals of different races. How, for instance, can a white counselor ask an African American client how she feels about being black if the counselor has no strong racial identity? It appears that many whites feel that a "color-blind" approach to life is the only viable nonracist position. However, a color-blind mind-set provides a rationale for counselors to avoid the cultural pain that a client of color may present.

DIFFERENCES BETWEEN RACE, CULTURE, AND CLASS

Counselors and clients often use *race*, *culture*, and *class* interchangeably. I define them as follows:

- Race: a genetic classification that is characterized by skin color, height, hair texture, eye shape, and eye color. There are only three races: Negroid, Caucasian, and Mongoloid.
- Culture: a term often associated with race but has a broader definition. For example, Hispanic culture encompasses all three races and numerous nationalities with many subgroups. Culture is often defined in terms of music, art, language, food, dress, humor, relationship between men and women, and so on.
- Class: an economic concept that refers to income, wealth, and social status.

Whites tend to define problems affecting African Americans in terms of culture or class. African Americans, on the other hand, tend to define problems in terms of race. As the diagram on page 33 illustrates, the more race is an issue between two individuals (one black, one white), the more power the African American has in the interaction. Few whites are willing to challenge the "authority" of African Americans on racial issues. One result of this is that whites tend to de-emphasize race and African Americans tend to overemphasize race, creating a significant amount of miscommunication.

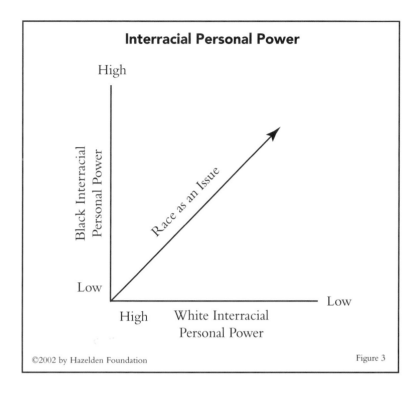

Interracial Personal Power

High

Black Interracial Personal Power

Race as an Issue

Low

Low

High   White Interracial Personal Power

©2002 by Hazelden Foundation

Figure 3

CULTURAL SCANNING

Cultural scanning is a practice of determining whether there is a racial or cultural aspect to a situation and, more important, how to appropriately respond to that situation.

Everyone has issues or topics that they are sensitive about. These can be based on personal traits, such as weight or baldness. Other sensitive issues or topics may be connected to societal stereotypes. For instance, a boundary may be crossed when a man talks about a woman who is blond but not very smart, or someone mentions a Jewish man who is truly tight with a dollar, or someone mentions a gay man who hates sports and is feminine.

Cultural/Racial Boundary Issues

1. Food
2. Humor
3. Hair
4. Crime
5. Sun tanning
6. Welfare
7. Unemployment/poverty
8. Athletics
9. Dancing
10. Music
11. Religion
12. Marriage/dating
13. Affirmative action
14. Politics
15. Housing/areas of town
16. Intelligence
17. Drugs
18. Mode of dress
19. Behavior/language
20. Racism

©2002 by Hazelden Foundation   Figure 4

There are many boundary issues for African Americans. These issues often develop from stereotypes and can elicit strong emotions. For example, many African Americans grew up hearing about "good hair" (straight) versus "bad hair" (kinky). As a counterbalance to this, Afros became a symbol of racial pride in the 1960s. Processed hair was and is often viewed as an example of latent self-hate. A disturbing superstition in American culture is that a white person can rub an African American's bald head to bring good luck. As a result of this history, cross-racial discussions regarding hair can cause anxiety for African Americans.

Another boundary issue for some African Americans is discussion of skin color. Many African Americans have experienced a white individual coming up to them after a vacation in the Caribbean, wanting to compare arms to see which individual is darker. This can create awkwardness and discomfort during which the African American doesn't quite know what to say or how to act.

Cultural boundary issues are fundamentally no different from gender, religious, or class boundaries. Learning how to cope with them, however, is an important racial identity development task in recovery.

Many women of any race often wonder what role gender plays in a first business encounter with a car mechanic. Questions often arise: "Does the mechanic take me seriously?" "Is he going to cheat me?" These questions often exist in a woman's mind even before she enters the garage. A similar thought process can take place when a woman negotiates the purchase of a car.

African Americans are often left wondering whether race played a role in many situations. Perhaps the best example is when an African American is stopped by the police. Another example is receiving poor service in a restaurant. Was the server just having a bad day, or was she displaying some degree of racial bias? If the teacher in a school disciplines an African American child, was it legitimate or was he acting on a racist stereotype? Did the boss dismiss someone's ideas because the ideas lacked creditability or because the person offering the ideas is African American?

Unfortunately, there are numerous examples of when race can be a partial or principal catalyst for a specific action. Most African Americans don't want to overreact and claim every slight as being caused by deep-seated racism. On the other hand, none of us wants to be disrespected or subjected to biased treatment. Balancing these two positions requires African Americans to be able to culturally scan a situation to determine the racial component and then fashion an appropriate response. In so doing, they must distinguish between ignorance, insensitivity, and racism.

The illustration on page 36 gives a visual sense of this process, which can be a major racial-identity recovery task.

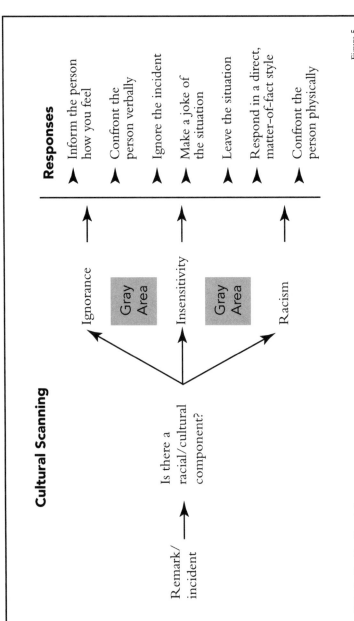

Cultural Scanning

Responses

Remark/ incident → Is there a racial/cultural component?

Ignorance → ▲ Inform the person how you feel

Gray Area → ▲ Confront the person verbally

→ ▲ Ignore the incident

Insensitivity → ▲ Make a joke of the situation

Gray Area → ▲ Leave the situation

→ ▲ Respond in a direct, matter-of-fact style

Racism → ▲ Confront the person physically

Figure 5

CULTURAL ADJUSTMENT ISSUES

Following is a description of cultural adjustment issues that many clients of color need to address to maximize the chances of a successful recovery.

Assimilation management is the process individuals of color go through to determine how they want to live in cultural terms. For instance, do they want to submerge themselves in their culture in both a work and social context? Will choice of food, music, clothes, neighborhood, religion, and dating and marriage partners all primarily reflect their culture? Must family members and friends be from their culture and support their choices and lifestyle? Or will they choose a more integrated path, one that allows some interplay among cultures, where one may work in one cultural environment and live in another? Often race and culture are important in marriage and religion but are less of an issue in terms of co-workers, business partners, or classmates. Or will they decide to become somewhat assimilated into the majority community, with patterns of speech and dress that are indistinguishable from the majority community?

All of the above choices regarding assimilation are legitimate, and all have pluses and minuses. The model on pages 38 and 39 illustrates the point. One exercise that is often done using the assimilation continuum is to request clients to put an *X* where they currently see themselves on the chart and a *Y* to illustrate a time in their life when they were furthest from the current location. Then, put an *F* for where their father is, an *M* for their mother, and an *S* to identify each sibling. This exercise, more than any other, illustrates the importance of varying degrees of assimilation by family members in a family system. The introspection this exercise demands can be enlightening for a client. A client can also be asked to place friends on the assimilation model and speculate where members of their racial group would place them. Here again, the possibilities for insight and growth are significant.

Assimilation Continuum

Separation	Integration	Assimilation
0	50	100
Pluses	Pluses	Pluses
Strong, positive cultural/racial identity	Linkage and appreciation of other communities and cultures	Viewed as special and different—"the good one"
Self-confident	Enhances career	Viewed as a pioneer
Less stress	Identified as a role model by many in community	Enhances career
Identified as a role model by many in community	Broader vision	Broader vision
Congruent, clear vision of the world	A bridge between cultures (moderator, interpreter)	Benefits from dominant culture
Strong acceptance by community of origin	Ability to benefit from numerous cultures	Seen as a role model by majority community
Viewed as a person with integrity and courage by community	Rigorous personal examination	Open to new ideas and cultural experiences
Strong sense of belonging	Speak for/represent race	Self-confident
Clear rules/norm	Viewed as a person with integrity and courage	Viewed by majority community as a person with integrity and courage
Secure and comfortable		

Figure 6

©2002 by Hazelden Foundation

Assimilation Continuum

Separation 0	Integration 50	Assimilation 100
Minuses	**Minuses**	**Minuses**
Suspicious of majority community	Pressure to choose	Racial/cultural self-doubt
Rationalizes inappropriate behavior	Feels inauthentic and disloyal	Viewed as a sellout
Limited appreciation of other cultures	Self-doubt	Unclear rules
Limits career	Identity conflict	Accepts some racist stereotypes
Overemphasize race/culture	Greater stress	Questions regarding depth and sincerity of acceptance by new community
Rigidity	Incongruent and changing values	Confusion/hostility from community/culture of origin
Tunnel vision	Family, friends, and co-workers are confused	No traditions and rituals
Appears angry	Viewed as two-faced and untrustworthy	Underemphasize race/culture
Intolerance of other racial/cultural groups	Always keeping a secret	Family conflicts
Viewed as negative role model by broader community	Speak for/represent race	Minimizes issues of racism and oppression
Exaggerated sense of culture of origin	Marginal sense of community	
Judges other individuals of color who have different views	Feels like a phony	
Viewed as out of touch and unrealistic		

Figure 6

Many cultural adjustment issues are very painful and buried quite deep. In and of themselves, these issues are no more important than concerns regarding sexuality, spirituality, or family issues. Their power often results from being painful secrets that don't get discussed in treatment or counseling. Addressing these issues can significantly improve the prospects for long-term recovery from chemical dependency. These issues include

- racial self-hate
- survivor's guilt
- racial loyalty
- racial authenticity
- sober fun
- emotional issues related to oppression

Racial Self-Hate

Racial self-hate is perhaps the most painful issue. It results from many African Americans' tendency to internalize the stereotypes seen in media and popular culture. One reflection of this is the fact that African Americans make many racist and insensitive statements toward each other.

The most vivid illustration is the color caste system that was prevalent in black America during and after slavery, and still exists to some degree today. Many black churches had a color code, which stipulated that you had to be a certain shade of black to be a member of the congregation. Complexion often affected the selection of a marriage partner. In effect, marrying darker was marrying down.

A white standard of beauty still exists today. One only has to look at African American music and movie stars to observe the point. The impact this has on an African American's self-perception is hard to overstate. How does an African American woman with strong

African features view herself in the face of this cultural assault? Does she have a safe place to talk about painful feelings resulting from a white standard of beauty? As mentioned earlier, it was not long ago in the black community when you heard discussions regarding "good hair" (straight) versus "bad hair" (kinky). Many African Americans report parents having preferences for children who had "white-like" features. In the 1950s, one could hear comments such as "The blacker the berry the sweeter the juice, too black the berry it ain't no use" and "If you're black get back, if you're brown stick around, if you're white you're all right."

Many African Americans feel a sense of shame or guilt regarding a perceived lack of progress made by their race. They often feel the need to explain or distance themselves from the African American community while not appearing disloyal. Virtually every African American is expected to have an "expert" opinion on all things black in the presence of whites. They are asked, in effect, to represent the race. This pressure and resulting emotional pain, while understandable and probably unavoidable, is rarely talked about as a part of the recovery process.

Survivor's Guilt

Many people in recovery feel a type of survivor's guilt, common in individuals who survive a plane crash or car accident. They wonder why they were chosen to live when others died. African Americans have similar feelings: *Why am I deserving of sobriety when so many of my family and friends are addicted, in jail, or dead?*

A similar dynamic is often associated with middle- and upper-income African Americans who are often criticized for "forgetting where they came from." This accusation is very devastating for many African Americans and can be used as an effective method of control by others. Many African Americans new to recovery often feel they are abandoning their family and friends and "selling out." If these feelings and thoughts are not addressed successfully, they can serve as relapse triggers where a person confuses alcohol and drug use with loyalty and commitment to old associates, family, and the African American community.

Racial Loyalty

A major aspect of recovery is sorting out loyalty issues. Answering the question "What does it mean to be loyal to family members, past drug-using friends, employers, co-workers, and those in recovery?" is important and often painful.

Many African Americans and other individuals of color also have racial loyalty issues that many whites simply don't understand. As mentioned above, some African Americans view recovery from addiction as a racially disloyal act. Other examples are internal conflicts from siding with a white co-worker in an argument against an African American co-worker, questioning the merits of affirmative action, or secretly enjoying hockey and classical music.

Issues of racial loyalty are often subtle but likely run deep, and they are rarely talked about in treatment. The accusation of being disloyal is a powerful tool of racial control in the African American community. This is particularly true for young people.

Racial Authenticity

Racial authenticity is similar to racial loyalty. A central goal of recovery is to find yourself and live an authentic life. Many African Americans define authenticity in primarily racial terms.

What does it mean to be authentically African American in America? Some African Americans define this by wearing African clothes and making pilgrimages to Africa. Others define this by segregating themselves in inner-city communities.

Is racial authenticity possible for African Americans who choose a more integrated lifestyle by living, working, and playing in a mixed racial environment? The issue of racial authenticity can have a significant impact on the choice of friends, career, partner, religious affiliation, and social activities. Addressing the issue of racial authenticity is very important for African Americans in recovery.

Sober Fun

A major aspect of recovery is learning to have sober fun. The fear of a joyless life can be a major block to recovery. Many addicts and alcoholics associate all things fun with their chemical of choice. They can't imagine laughing, enjoying a walk with a friend, or attending a sporting event without their chemical of choice.

This issue also has a significant cultural dimension. Black humor in many ways is different from white humor. All one has to do is listen to an African American comic or watch Black Entertainment Television (BET) to understand the point. Many counselors are uncomfortable and unfamiliar with black humor and associate it with a "street lifestyle." As a result, it can be subtly discouraged. This often sends the message to African American clients in treatment that acculturation is a prerequisite to recovery.

A second issue is that play in America is often a segregated activity, whether it is a card game or a jazz concert. Few African Americans would feel comfortable taking a white friend to a gospel concert. A challenge for African American clients is learning how to have sober fun in a comfortable cultural environment.

Emotional Issues Related to Oppression

Individuals of color have essentially four responses to oppression. The illustration on page 44 outlines the options.

Response Options to Oppression

(Victim)	(Survivor/Crusader)
I'm not okay because society will not or cannot change.	I'm okay but society must change for others to be okay.
(Self-Hate)	(Self-Actualization)
I'm not okay and I must change to be accepted by society.	I'm okay whether or not society ever changes.

©2002 by Hazelden Foundation

Figure 7

Victim

This position essentially says "I'm not okay—in my job, school, family, finances, self-esteem, and so on. Racism and prejudice in society is principally or largely to blame." In other words, society needs to change before the individual can be successful in major areas of life.

Counselors confronted with the victim stance need to point out how the client is giving society the power to virtually control his or her life. This client needs to assess the things he or she can control and come to an acceptance of the things that are beyond his or her reach. In effect, the client needs to come to an appreciation of the Serenity Prayer: *God grant me the serenity to accept the things I cannot change, the courage to change the things I can, and the wisdom to know the difference.*

Survivor/crusader

These individuals view themselves as having survived in spite of significant obstacles in their paths. They often raise significant concerns regarding the lack of progress on racial issues in the United States. In many respects, they view themselves as spokespeople for or protectors of the "victim group," of which they are a part. As with the victim group, counseling sessions can get politicized. Clients may experience some survivor's guilt as a result of any successes they have achieved in life.

Self-hate

These individuals view themselves as failures and tend to blame themselves rather than society for any of their shortcomings. They will often dismiss or minimize discussions regarding racism and oppression. This position is somewhat naive. Racism is a fact of life that does affect a person's prospects for employment, housing, health care, education, and so on. The goal is to weigh accurately the effects of racism against a client's responsibility for taking initiative in key areas of life.

Self-actualization

This is the desired position for a client to reach. These clients do not deny the existence of racism; they just refuse to be controlled or limited by it. They have found a way to reach a sense of personal acceptance regardless of how the larger world views them. They don't carry a chip on their shoulder or look at every setback as having a racial basis. Often, they have developed sophisticated cultural survival skills that help them function in a variety of environments.

STAGES OF ADOLESCENT RACIAL AWARENESS

Racial awareness is a significant issue when treating African American adolescents. It is commonly accepted that chemical dependency retards adolescent development and that treatment is in many respects a crash course in maturation. Adolescence is a time when young people make important decisions regarding their sexuality, spirituality, and career. It is also a time when African Americans increasingly develop their racial identity.

When individuals go through treatment, they often must address issues that were previously medicated and unresolved. The following chart illustrates the various stages of racial awareness from infancy to young adulthood.

Stages of Racial Development

Age

2–4 Becomes aware of overt physical difference, such as size, shape, and skin color.

5–8 Begins to form self-image via media portrayals of racial minorities and the emphasis on a white standard of beauty.

9–11 Becomes aware of differences and develops stereotypes associated with race in school performance, behavior, sports, and so on.

12–15 Becomes aware of the role race plays in the social dynamics of friendship, dating, and so on. Social groups form. Issues of racial loyalty and authenticity develop.

16–18 Becomes aware of the role race plays in crime, unemployment, voting patterns, and other political and economic situations.

Over 18 Develops racial and cultural social competencies to know what to say to whom. Establishes cultural boundaries. Learns how to scan situations to determine the racial and cultural dynamics.

©2002 by Hazelden Foundation   Figure 8

CULTURAL STEREOTYPES

Stereotypes can be viewed as expectations that society places on an individual. As with other expectations, we respond in a number of ways, ranging from living up to them to rebelling against them. In addition, stereotypes can cause African Americans to be suspicious of the actions of others. Are motives pure or based on a bias or stereotype? Sorting through these issues can be a major racial identity recovery task.

How African Americans respond to stereotypes is a complex and painful issue. In many respects, stereotypes are the application of statistics to a population in a hurried world. Many blacks excel in certain sports: basketball, football, track, and boxing. Many African Americans also excel in music and entertainment. On the other hand, few African Americans are known in the physical sciences or math. They are also underrepresented as physicians and lawyers. Most disturbing of all is the significant overrepresentation of African Americans as inmates in the criminal justice system. The impact these facts and the resulting stereotypes have on the emotional lives of African Americans is hard to overstate. Many African Americans spend considerable energy living up to or attempting to refute the myriad of stereotypes that others have of them. Equally important is the fact that many African Americans have internalized society's stereotypes of them.

This can result in a form of *stereotype anxiety*. If society views a group as smart or dumb, hardworking or lazy, good or poor athletes, members of that group will likely respond to those expectations. For example, an African American boy who is not a good athlete may feel a measure of shame. He may come to view himself as having less worth because he is not living up to the expectations of others. Mid-level African American managers may be very sensitive to supervisors or co-workers who do not seem to respect their ideas and input at team meetings. They may feel others are stereotyping them as not having the same intellectual gifts as their co-workers. They may view small slights as examples of deep-seated disrespect and unfair stereo-typing.

Whether true or not, both of these examples reflect a measure of cultural pain that can affect a person's self-perception and relation-ships with others.

Chapter 4

African American Subgroups and Counseling Issues

A way to understand the issue of assimilation in the African American community is to view the various subgroups that exist within that community. Four major subgroups currently exist in the African American community:

- acculturated
- bicultural
- culturally immersed
- traditional unacculturated

It is important to understand these groups in a historical context. From the time of slavery to the 1960s, both African American and white communities expected the African American community to attempt to gain some degree of acculturation. In other words, it was expected that African Americans would assume the values, norms, and behaviors of whites.

In the 1960s, acculturation was challenged. Large segments of the African American community rejected acculturation in favor of a more Afrocentric view. This was the era of "black is beautiful" that ushered in hairstyles and clothing which demonstrated a pride in what is unique to African American individuals. This was also the era

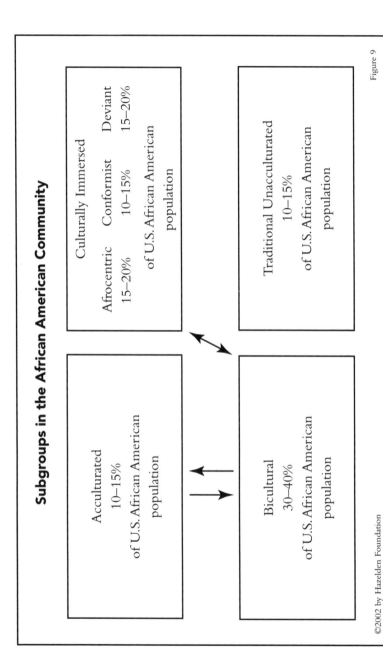

Subgroups in the African American Community

Acculturated
10–15%
of U.S. African American population

Bicultural
30–40%
of U.S. African American population

Culturally Immersed

Afrocentric   Conformist   Deviant
15–20%   10–15%   15–20%
of U.S. African American population

Traditional Unacculturated
10–15%
of U.S. African American population

Figure 9

of major clashes in inner-city African American neighborhoods, demonstrations, civil disobedience, looting, and other forms of social disorder.

The upheavals of the late 1960s and early 1970s created a great deal of consternation between the differing groups in the African American community. That consternation can still be observed in some educational and civil rights organizations today.

Each African American needs to decide which profile is best for himself or herself. As a rule, whites are most comfortable with acculturated African Americans. In the chart on page 50, I estimate percentages of African Americans that fall into each category. These estimates are based on my own work and observations and would be difficult to quantify in a scientific manner.

ACCULTURATED

The acculturated African American individual has made a conscious decision to live, work, and play outside of the African American community. Acculturated African Americans tend to reflect very few African American mannerisms in dress or speech. They are usually well educated. (Historically, one by-product of education has been acculturation.) Because of their education, these African Americans are often employed in mid- to upper-management positions in both the private and public sectors. This group represents approximately 10 to 15 percent of the African American population.

Acculturated African Americans tend to be critical of other African Americans who don't "pull themselves up by their bootstraps." As a group, they tend to reject, minimize, or give lip service to the impact of racism on the African American community. They are highly skilled in their interaction with whites. In fact, they are often more skilled at communicating and functioning with whites than with other African Americans.

The interests and identifying characteristics of acculturated African Americans are closely linked to the white community. This includes, for example, their choices of clothing, food, art, music, and entertainment. They get both their personal needs (relationships, spirituality, and recreation) and survival needs (employment, education, and political affiliation) met in a white societal context.

Acculturated African Americans usually have developed strong emotional defense systems. This group is often the least likely to be treated for chemical dependency because of its sophisticated ability to manipulate the system. A key to intervention with people in this group is to illustrate the impact their chemical use has on their way of life or their standing in the white community.

The following observations may be helpful to counselors, in order to provide effective treatment to acculturated African Americans:

- They get much of their self-worth and identity from being able to function and interact in an all-white setting. The acculturated African American's view of himself or herself is significantly reinforced and heightened through acceptance by whites. Acculturated African Americans often talk about where they were educated, cultural events they like, and other topics that disassociate them from the black community.

- Acculturated African Americans often enter into an unspoken contract with whites for mutual acceptance. Many white individuals, in an effort to establish that they are open-minded and harbor few racial biases, seek relationships with African Americans and other members of minority groups. They often quickly mention to an African American past interactions they have had with other African Americans. This need by white individuals to establish personal credibility can have a significant effect on therapy. The African American (often acculturated) who offers acceptance to a white counselor has a kind of power—cultural seduction—that is often used in a manipulative way.

The other three categories of African Americans look at the acculturated group with a degree of contempt and anger. But that view is balanced by a degree of respect for the economic and educational advances of the individual.

African Americans from other groups may attempt to exploit any deep-seated guilt feelings the acculturated African American may have as a result of having "left" the African American community. This dynamic is particularly evident in counseling situations where the counselor is an acculturated African American and the client is from one of the other three categories. In effect, clients may play on racial loyalty issues with the counselors in order to receive preferential treatment.

It is particularly important for white individuals to understand that while the African Americans they know, such as neighbors and co-workers, are more likely to be acculturated, the number of acculturated African Americans is relatively small. The white community knows the African American community from two primary sources: acculturated African Americans and the media. This gives the white community a somewhat distorted perception of what the entire African American community is really like.

BICULTURAL

Bicultural African Americans have the ability to function and interact within both the African American and the white communities. Often, however, they feel somewhat unaccepted in both. They have a sense of pride, which is not defensive, regarding their racial identity. They often respect and appreciate other cultural groups. This group represents approximately 30 to 40 percent of the African American community and is probably growing most rapidly.

In a very real sense, the bicultural African American is bilingual, having the ability to communicate in "standard English" but also having the ability and comfort to relate to the "brothers on the street," often using African American dialect in the process.

The bicultural African American's personal tastes as reflected in choices of clothing, entertainment, art, and music are a mixture of activities and actions accepted in both the African American and white communities. Bicultural African Americans often achieve the same educational level as acculturated African Americans.

Bicultural African Americans get their personal needs met in both an African American and a white context but rarely in an integrated one. They might, for example, go to a party with their white co-workers and have enjoyable experiences comfortably interacting with everyone. They could also attend a party with African American friends and enjoy themselves to an equal degree. But they would have trouble if the two parties were held together; this would produce a major role conflict. The dilemma the bicultural individual would face is *Which role should I play? Which dialect and image should I use? What will each group think of me as I move outside each group's perception of me?*

Bicultural African Americans experience role conflict when they are with a group of white friends and encounter an African American friend who speaks in an African American dialect, or conversely, if they are with African American friends and they encounter a white friend or co-worker. This role conflict can be a significant source of emotional discomfort for bicultural African Americans.

When white individuals develop close relationships with bicultural African Americans, they may sometimes feel confused. In close relationships, there is typically a great deal of emotional sharing and a sense of understanding the other person. When the white individual sees the African American friend in an African American context, he or she may feel confusion and a sense of betrayal because of the different persona the African American may assume. The white individual may also perceive discomfort from the African American friend. The white individual thinks, *I thought I knew you. I thought we could talk and share everything. Now I see this entirely different side of you, one that I don't understand and am somewhat uncomfortable with.*

The bicultural African American may also confuse others in the African American community. The acculturated African American may avoid the bicultural person because of that person's sense of African American identity. The other groups of African Americans are uneasy or unclear about the bicultural person's ability to and interest in interacting with whites.

The bicultural African American's survival needs are met in a predominantly white context. The educational level achieved, work experience, and political affiliation of the bicultural individual are all within "acceptable norms" of white America. Bicultural African Americans place a strong value in climbing the economic ladder but not at the expense of their racial identity.

A problem bicultural African American individuals face in recovery is that when they enter treatment, they often assume the role of the acculturated. In essence, that is the context in which they achieve their sobriety. When they leave treatment, they need to maintain their sobriety as they truly are, which is bicultural and not acculturated. This reality can cause significant problems.

In many respects, bicultural African Americans are the bridge between the African American community and the white community. Bicultural individuals often view themselves in this manner and take great pride in this role. Their ability to communicate, work, and function in two different worlds produces a great deal of pride but also causes considerable confusion and pain. This "cultural schizophrenia," or role conflict, is an important issue to address in recovery. Just verbalizing the dilemma and realizing that they are not alone or abnormal often reduces the stress felt by bicultural African Americans.

CULTURALLY IMMERSED

Culturally immersed African Americans can be divided into three subgroups:

- culturally immersed conformists
- culturally immersed Afrocentrics
- culturally immersed deviants

The unifying characteristic of the three is the choice to live apart from the white community. They represent perhaps 40 to 55 percent of the African American community. If you went into one of their homes, you would clearly know you were in the home of an African American. The art on the wall and music on the stereo would all reflect the cultural identity of the group. Combined they are perhaps the largest group in the African American community. While these subgroups often live in close proximity to each other, they have little social interaction with each other.

Culturally Immersed Conformists (CICs)

Culturally immersed conformists have a strong sense of themselves as African American individuals. They were raised and continue to live in predominantly African American communities.

CICs have their survival needs met in a white context. The CIC is usually a high school graduate and works in relatively high-paying trades or in factories. CICs' interaction with whites, however, is generally limited to the workplace. While they have the ability to interact with whites in a work environment, they are uncomfortable socializing with whites outside that context. They have little interaction with acculturated African Americans and are somewhat amused by them. Their interaction with the rest of the African American community is varied.

Culturally immersed conformists get their personal needs met in an exclusively African American context. Their choices of music, clothing, art, and entertainment are all strongly identified with the African American community.

While CICs tend to work in traditional jobs, they often socialize with other African Americans who may be unemployed, involved in illegal activities, or both. There is a segment of the African American community that moves from legitimate work to illegal activities with relative ease.

CICs tend to respond well to treatment, though they are prone to using humor as a defense. While experiencing no more racial self-hate than any of the other subgroups, they tend to engage in "in group" racial put-downs. Growing up and living in primarily African American neighborhoods, they have often played "the dozens" (a shame-based form of humor based on physical appearance and ridicule of family members). It is sometimes challenging for white counselors or acculturated African American counselors not to overreact to this humor and to see it as a part of their addiction.

One major block to successful long-term recovery with individuals in this group is the significant challenge they face in learning how to have sober fun. A second block to long-term recovery is their social interaction with African Americans who are involved in illegal activities, which often includes using and selling drugs.

Culturally Immersed Afrocentrics (CIAs)

Culturally immersed Afrocentrics, in many respects, serve as the new black intelligentsia. Afrocentrics tend to be well educated, articulate, and self-confident. They are often employed by social service agencies or in academia.

The driving force in CIAs' lives is to build a politically powerful and economically independent African American community. CIAs are often contemptuous of whites and even more so of acculturated African Americans.

CIAs tend to politicize most social issues, including chemical dependency. They view racism as the primary factor for most inappropriate and dysfunctional behaviors in the African American community. Viewing addiction as a primary illness is difficult for them. They see it, instead, as a secondary symptom of racism and oppression.

According to CIAs, any treatment strategy that doesn't incorporate the theme of racism and oppression at its core is ineffective and possibly damaging. When whites attempt to counsel CIAs, sessions either deteriorate into a series of power plays or tend to get politicized.

The cultural identity of CIAs is strongly associated with black Africa. This is reflected in their choices of music, art, literature, and clothing. CIAs fulfill their personal needs in an exclusively African American context. They also meet many of their survival needs in the African American community. Many of them are aligned formally or informally with Islam.

CIAs have one of the lowest rates of chemical dependency in the country. This may be due to the fact that they are involved with something greater than themselves and feel a sense of mission that provides them with some degree of immunity from alcohol and drug abuse. Although they are small in number, CIAs exert a significant influence on the African American community.

Culturally Immersed Deviants (CIDs)

Culturally immersed deviants are the group of African Americans that the white community finds most intimidating. They have been labeled by the media as the "underclass" and are likely to be involved in criminal activities. Often, CIDs were raised in single-parent households, lived in public housing, are functionally illiterate, and hold a survival-of-the-fittest worldview. They have little interaction with whites.

CIDs are contemptuous of whites and acculturated African Americans, and tend to see both groups as potential targets for their illegal activities. They tend to view everyone as engaged in one form of hustle or another. As a group, CIDs are more prone to polydrug, opiate, and crack use, all heavily laced with alcohol consumption. CIDs speak the urban black dialect. Their personal needs get met exclusively in the African American community, and their survival needs are also primarily met in the African American community.

Treatment is extremely difficult for this group because their values and goals are so far removed from mainstream American culture. Long-term or more intensive therapy is often required. Culturally relevant treatment is often the most effective treatment strategy.

As a result of their belief that no one is honest or engaged in legitimate activities, CIDs have difficulty accepting an African American counselor as being competent and sincere. They may perceive both counselors and the treatment or aftercare agency as nothing more than a sophisticated hustle. They will doubt that the agency really is what it says it is, suspecting instead that it is somehow conning individuals and getting money illegitimately. This projection by CIDs of their own values on counselors can present a major challenge to recovery.

Most often, CIDs find their way into a methadone maintenance clinic or a nonabstinence-based therapeutic community. Problems often arise in aftercare because these individuals have so few coping skills and minimal support from the community.

CICs, CIAs, and CIDs must go through a process of "exempting" a white therapist before allowing that individual to help them. In other words, they need to view the white therapist as different from other white individuals or as the exception rather than the rule. This process legitimizes the white individual and allows the culturally immersed African American to interact positively with a non-black individual.

A culturally immersed African American will generally have more difficulty exempting an acculturated African American counselor than a white counselor. The acculturated African American may be viewed as having turned on his or her race, and this can make the exemption process more difficult.

TRADITIONAL UNACCULTURATED

People in the traditional unacculturated group have a very strong Christian spiritual base that would be easy to observe if one went into their homes. Their taste in music, art, literature, and entertainment is all deeply affected by religion and spirituality.

Traditional unacculturated African Americans tend to be older, live in the South, and speak the southern rural African American dialect. They are a decreasing segment of the African American community. They are the parents of much of the African American community and are respected by virtually everyone, but they only represent approximately 10 to 15 percent of the African American community.

Members of this group are sometimes victimized by crime perpetrated by other African Americans, yet they often protect the predators. They are proud of the acculturated group of African Americans but feel alienated and resentful of how acculturated African Americans view them as outdated, unsophisticated, and ignorant.

Traditional unacculturated African Americans get their survival needs met in a white context, but their personal needs are met in an exclusively African American context. Historically, they value integration but not assimilation. They feel African Americans should aspire to work with whites on an equal level, but not socialize with whites for fear of losing the rich African American cultural identity.

Important counseling points come from a review of these four profiles.

- These categories are very fluid. African American individuals choose to participate in any one of them because of what they perceive to be necessary for their emotional and physical survival. An African American may be raised as acculturated, go to college and take on the viewpoints or beliefs of one of the other subgroups and then, after graduation, move into the work world and become bicultural. An African American can also assume different roles with different individuals and different settings. With a group of African American friends, an individual might assume one role; with white co-workers, that same individual might assume another role.
- These groups must be viewed in a nonjudgmental context. The goal of counseling should not be to move a client from one group to another group, but rather to help a client locate himself or herself in whatever group he or she identifies with and to explore the positives and negatives of membership in that group.
- White counselors may or may not be able to counsel African American individuals on many of the problems each subgroup experiences. This ability depends on the extent to which white

counselors understand the issues and feel comfortable with them. Being aware of the different subgroups of African Americans is only a first step in understanding. White counselors who wish to broaden their abilities to counsel African American clients would do well to go to African American cultural events, such as a service at an African American church. They may also learn about African American culture by reading novels written by African American authors and going to plays written by African American playwrights.

At first a white individual can anticipate feeling alienated and uncomfortable, but if the individual is sincere and continues trying, he or she will gradually develop an appreciation for different experiences, worldviews, and values that exist in the African American culture. One of the most significant experiences a white individual can have by attending events in the African American community is increased color consciousness, by virtue of being a minority there.

CHAPTER 5

Responding to Differences

Our response to cultural differences is determined by many factors, including our parents' views of different groups, our religious upbringing, and personal experience. Answering the following eight questions will provide insight into what shapes our individual response to cultural differences:

- What personal experiences have you had with individuals from different cultures, and how have they shaped your views? Are your experiences limited? Were they good, bad, or a mixture of both?
- What religious or moral tenets were you taught growing up regarding different cultures? How did your parents, friends, and religious institutions view other groups?
- What peer group expectations currently exist regarding your treatment of different groups? Are you expected to show sensitivity? Bias? Indifference?
- What similarities do you or persons close to you share with different cultures? When you were growing up, did you have an uncle, aunt, or other close relative who was gay but secretive about it? Has a family member or friend married or adopted across racial lines? How has that worked out?

- Do you think different cultures have a measure of control over what makes them different? For instance, do you think African Americans as a group should take on more "middle-class" values? Or do you think all immigrants into the United States should learn to speak English?
- How do media and popular culture portray different cultures? Do media reinforce or break down stereotypes, or are media oversensitive to them?
- What legal mandates exist regarding treatment of different cultures and how does that affect your behavior?
- Do you perceive different cultures to be a direct or indirect threat in a financial, social, or cultural context? Do you feel threatened, that a group is taking over your community, school, or city? Do you think a group has gained undue benefit from its status as a different group?

COUNSELOR RESPONSES TO DIFFERENCES

How counselors can best respond to differences in others is an important issue. Counselors often fool themselves into believing that they treat everyone the same. The fact is *all* counselors respond to differences in a variety of ways. In fact, counselors respond very differently to a person based on his or her age, sex, race, or religion. It is only through recognizing their feelings about a particular difference that counselors can gain a measure of control over their responses. The following list identifies five responses counselors can have to a difference:

- bias or insensitivity
- minimizing, ignoring, or denying
- toleration
- oversensitivity or overresponse
- valuing and acceptance

Bias or Insensitivity

One response to differences is bias or insensitivity. This response is often characterized by

- seeing the difference as generally negative
- seeing the difference as being used to excuse questionable behavior
- seeing the difference as illegitimate or unnatural
- making and accepting stereotypical remarks regarding the persons with the difference
- avoiding associations with individuals who embody that difference
- attempting to convert or change individuals who represent the difference

Counselors who are biased or insensitive to a specific difference often make the following types of comments:

- "Why don't those people change their ways?"
- "I don't care what anyone thinks; I am just telling the truth about those people."
- "There are certain values, standards, and traditions we have to maintain."
- "We can't have everyone just doing their own thing."
- "Oil and water just don't mix."

Minimizing, Ignoring, or Denying

The second response to differences is to minimize, ignore, or deny. This is characterized by

- feeling threatened by the difference in question

- showing conditional acceptance based on denial and a mutual conspiracy of silence with the client
- fearing that emphasizing the difference will be divisive

Counselors who minimize, ignore, or deny differences often make the following types of comments:

- "People are people."
- "I treat everyone the same."
- "There is only one race: the human race."
- "All people bleed red blood."
- "I wasn't raised like that."
- "We should celebrate our similarities, not our differences."
- "We all want the same things."
- "We all have to put our differences aside and come together."
- "Why can't we just all get along?"

Toleration

The third response to differences is toleration. This position is characterized by

- not being threatened by the difference, by viewing it as somewhat neutral
- not attempting to convert or change the client, but also not truly accepting the difference
- viewing the difference as beyond the control of the individual or of little to no importance
- viewing the difference as permissible but not equal

Counselors who tolerate a specific difference make the following types of comments:

- "They have a right to lead their lives if they don't bother anyone."
- "I can live with them."
- "All groups have some good and some bad."
- "They have a right to a job and education just like everyone else."
- "I don't like what they do, but they have a right to do it."
- "Nobody's perfect."
- "I don't want to impose my values and standards on them."

Oversensitivity or Overresponse

The fourth response to differences is oversensitivity or overresponse. This is often viewed as being "politically correct" and is characterized by

- overresponding to the difference in question
- emphasizing a person's differences over other, more numerous similarities
- hesitation to criticize questionable actions for fear of being accused of insensitivity
- allowing differences to be used as excuses
- tending to put down their own group as abusive, elitist, or racist

Counselors who are oversensitive to differences often make the following types of comments:

- "How can I question or judge another group?"
- "All cultural groups have a right to do what they want."
- "I don't know what you expect—their group is devastated by whites."
- "Those aren't lower standards, just different standards."

Valuing and Acceptance

The fifth response truly values and accepts the difference in question. This position is characterized by

- accepting a specific difference without allowing that difference to be used as an excuse
- recognizing both strengths and weaknesses of different cultural and racial groups
- valuing input and stimulation from a wide range of groups
- understanding that all racial and cultural groups have similar values that are uniquely expressed

Counselors who truly value and accept differences make these types of comments:

- "There are more similarities between people, but we can't discount the differences."
- "We must get input from a wide range of views."
- "I like having my ideas and views challenged."
- "I think those individuals are using their racial and cultural background to protect themselves from criticism."

Please refer to the "Responses to Diversity Questionnaire" on page 117 to gain insight into how individuals respond to differences. In addition, the matrix titled "Importance of Diversity in Relationships" (page 110) can help individuals gauge their attitudes toward differences.

CHAPTER 6

Cultural Considerations in Alcohol and Drug Abuse Prevention Services

A number of years ago, psychologist Abraham Maslow developed a hierarchy of needs. His model illustrates how human needs are sequentially met. He believed that basic needs such as safety and security must be addressed before needs such as food, clothing, and shelter, and significantly before issues such as a sense of belonging or self-actualization. This model can be adapted to show how communities or individuals have a hierarchy of responses to alcohol and other drug abuse, based on the perceived needs in the respective communities or families.

As the model illustrates, an individual or community will likely have personal safety and security as its first concern. Any efforts regarding prevention or treatment will likely be ineffective if there are significant safety concerns resulting from alcohol and drug use in a person's home or community. In these situations, communities often demand increased police protection, community watch programs, or orders of protection.

Only after a community or individual feels somewhat secure from the instability caused by crime will treatment be an option. A community is similar to a family member who is battered by an alcohol-abusing spouse. Only when safe from further physical abuse will the battered individual attempt to secure help for the alcohol abuser.

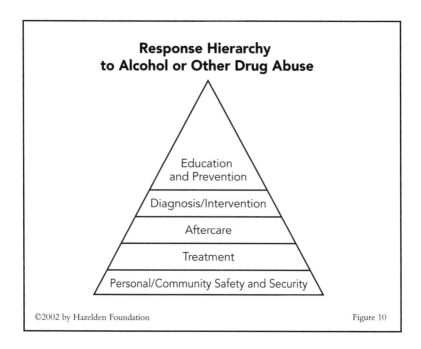

**Response Hierarchy
to Alcohol or Other Drug Abuse**

Education
and Prevention

Diagnosis/Intervention

Aftercare

Treatment

Personal/Community Safety and Security

©2002 by Hazelden Foundation

Figure 10

This is due to the fact that alcohol and drug abuse treatment is the most compelling service in our nation's continuum of care, which also includes detoxification, education, prevention, intervention, and aftercare. As the old saying goes, "The squeaky wheel gets the oil." Untreated alcohol and drug abusers are very visible in our communities and families and tend to cause great havoc. But when these individuals are successfully treated, they can become a strong force of good and inspiration.

After members of a community start to see treatment services as effective and available, they usually become interested in the development of other elements of the continuum of care, namely, aftercare services and early intervention services. These can be viewed as cost-effective methods of making treatment more effective.

Finally, a community or individual focuses on education and prevention efforts last, not because these services are less important, but because they are less compelling and harder to define. Most people don't think they need additional education about drug use and treatment. Many believe they know how treatment works through personal stories of a family member, friend, or co-worker.

Prevention, on the other hand, is a series of activities that are established to discourage a behavior. Identifying a connection between an individual's treatment and an improvement in his or her quality of life is much easier and more visible than the connection between a school prevention curriculum taught to a child who is ten years old and his or her choice not to use alcohol or drugs at sixteen years old. Unfortunately, this reality places prevention services at a competitive disadvantage in securing funding support from government and philanthropic sources.

CURRENT PREVENTION STRATEGIES

There are two major prevention strategies used in the United States today: social competency prevention and social policy prevention.

Social Competency Prevention

Social competency prevention is the reduction of alcohol and drug abuse in youths by the development of skills and knowledge essential to day-to-day living:

- clear values
- effective emotional coping skills
- effective decision-making skills
- alternative activities
- communication skills
- refusal skills

The delivery system for this model of prevention has primarily been schools via the use of curricula.

A number of concerns surround social competency prevention. The first is its focus on youths. Many believe that, while adolescence is the time of highest risk, it is not the only time of risk—the mid-forties are another, and the mid-sixties a third. Prevention messages should be given throughout the life cycle. In addition, there may be a need to develop *event-specific prevention*. These prevention messages are tied to traumatic or transitional life events, such as the death of a spouse, the loss of a job, moving to a new community, starting college, or retirement.

A second concern is social competency prevention's emphasis on alternative highs. Feeling hurt, lonely, bored, frustrated, or angry is a part of life. Critics of social competency prevention say that prevention should focus more on accepting those feelings as part of the human condition rather than ameliorating them.

A third concern is having schools as the primary delivery system for prevention services. Individuals most in need of prevention services are often not in school. In many instances they have dropped out or are truant. As a result, prevention agencies should look toward recreational facilities, juvenile justice centers, churches, and similar access points to deliver their much-needed services.

Prevention specialists also know that the highest risk group for alcohol and drug addiction is the children of addicts and alcoholics. Consideration should be given to pilot testing prevention programs in treatment centers targeting the children of clients receiving care.

Social Policy Prevention

The second form of prevention is social policy, defined as the establishment and communication of functional norms, standards, and consequences that are culturally relevant regarding alcohol and drug use and abuse.

This strategy of prevention has been widely used to prevent tobacco use but has been emphasized less in preventing alcohol and drug abuse. The approach rests on six questions that all cultures, communities, families, and individuals answer in one form or another:

- What chemicals are legitimate to use?
- Has the culture, community, or family established a context for chemical use?
- Are there cultural institutions that can effectively establish and communicate alcohol- and other drug-use rules?
- Are there clear cultural, community, or family systems of accountability?
- Are there functional tools to cope with stress?
- Are there functional rites of passage?

When these questions get answered clearly, fewer alcohol and drug problems occur. Very clear cultural rules regarding alcohol and other drugs are common to groups of individuals with low rates of chemical abuse. These groups include Native Americans two centuries ago and Orthodox Jews and Mormons today.

What chemicals are legitimate to use?

In American society, rules regarding alcohol and other drugs have broken down. The 1960s ushered in an era of challenge to old rules and authority. Among those rules challenged, especially by young people, was the taboo on all drugs except alcohol. Marijuana became popular among college students who rejected their parents' assumption that alcohol was the only acceptable recreational drug. Marijuana, while still illegal, has since gained a more acceptable status than other drugs. A collapse of clear taboos on a drug tends to facilitate its abuse.

The breakdown of social taboos regarding drugs has been followed by efforts to legalize them. Advocates for this approach maintain that legalizing all drugs will eliminate the lucrative criminal industry that currently manufactures and distributes them.

The problem with legalization is that when a drug is legalized or otherwise culturally legitimized, more individuals will use it. When more individuals use a specific chemical, more will become abusers and addicted, thereby causing harm to themselves, their families, and society. Many argue that, with alcohol, there is already enough crime, domestic violence, divorce, unemployment, and poorly planned pregnancies. We must ask ourselves, *Can society afford to legalize and therefore expand the use of other psychoactive substances?*

Some advocates of legalization operate under the false assumption that all chemicals have the same addictive potential. While only one in ten individuals may use alcohol to excess, a far greater percentage of crack users will become dependent on this highly addictive substance.

The United States would be well served if the field of chemical dependency followed the lead of current antismoking efforts. We are observing the delegitimization of tobacco in our society. We literally see the signs all around us. They include no-smoking sections in restaurants, a smoking ban on airline flights, no-smoking hotel rooms, and a ban on tobacco ads on radio and television. Few among us now associate tobacco use with glamour.

Has the culture, community, or family established a context for chemical use?

When is it legitimate to use alcohol or other drugs? What behaviors should we tolerate from those who use alcohol and other drugs? The clearer the answers to these questions, the fewer alcohol and other drug problems a society will have. Historically, there are three culturally established reasons for the use of mood-altering chemicals. The first is for ritualistic or ceremonial events, usually tied to religious rites or worship. The second is for medicinal purposes. The third is for festive, celebratory occasions.

Today, American culture has validated a number of new reasons for alcohol and other drug use. One is the use of alcohol and other drugs as a social lubricant to facilitate camaraderie, to help individuals relax and enjoy themselves. This may have grown out of, but is not the same as, the aforementioned festive occasions. Festive or celebratory occasions, such as when the harvest is in, traditionally occurred only once or twice a year rather than on a daily or weekly basis.

American society seems to be going in two different directions regarding where chemicals should be used and what behaviors should be tolerated. On the positive side, driving while under the influence is less tolerated today than twenty years ago. On the negative side, many believe that popular culture—as reflected by many rap and rock songs—glorifies alcohol and drug abuse and inappropriate behavior.

The breakdown of old rules regarding chemical use is nowhere more apparent than in our schools. Using or being under the influence of drugs is prohibited in schools, but it is often tolerated because the magnitude of the problem is far greater than the staff can handle. This sends confusing messages to young people. They are told that use is forbidden in school, but they see many of their peers clearly under the influence of drugs and getting by with it.

Native American communities of the past and Jewish communities of the present are instructive. Both groups establish clear cultural norms for chemical use. Chemicals are used in a family or communal setting and imbedded in religious tradition.

Are there cultural institutions that can effectively establish and communicate alcohol- and other drug-use rules?

This is where American culture has changed the most. Historically, there were three institutions that established chemical use and abuse rules: religious organizations, the family, and the state. While these three groups continue to exert significant influence, the liquor industry is a strong counterforce that seeks to legitimize alcohol consumption and establish norms regarding alcohol use. The liquor industry does this through its multibillion-dollar marketing efforts that include massive advertising campaigns specifically targeting African American individuals and communities. Rarely is there an African American or Hispanic cultural or musical event that does not have the liquor or tobacco industry as a major sponsor.

The liquor industry argues that the purpose of these ads is to ensure brand loyalty, not to increase consumption. We must keep in mind, however, that a small percentage of our nation's overall population consumes a high percentage of alcohol. "Beer consumed by the highest tenth percentile of drinkers by volume represents 42 percent of the reported alcohol consumed in the United States."[1]

Federal government studies indicate that the younger the age of drinking onset, the greater the chance that the individual will develop a drinking problem at some point in his or her life. Young people who began drinking before age fifteen were four times more likely to develop alcoholism than those who began drinking at age twenty-one.[2] This creates a strong incentive for the liquor industry to market its products toward the nation's youths, a large percentage of which are minorities. Colorful, youth-oriented packaging on alcoholic drinks is formulated to appeal to young people, including teenagers, who often do not like the taste of alcohol. These "alco-pops" pave the way to more common alcoholic beverages.[3]

Liquor advertisements on television reach a disproportionate number of African Americans. "African-Americans are the largest minority segment of the U.S. television household population, comprising approximately 12 percent of the 102 million TV households. African-Americans generally watch more television than other segments of the population."[4]

Liquor industry efforts targeted at African Americans include

- inner-city billboards
- ads in African American–oriented magazines
- television commercials that use African American athletes to endorse products
- sponsorship of rock concerts and other musical events

The liquor industry tries to associate social equality and African American pride with its products. African American drinkers are often portrayed as sophisticated, upscale members of society. The goal is to link African American drinkers with financial success. Many African American–oriented magazines are heavily dependent on liquor ads for revenue, and unfortunately, few articles in these magazines address the problem of alcoholism in the African American community.

The saturation of advertising in the African American community, as well as the evidence that African American individuals respond more readily to advertising, is more than a little disquieting.

Are there clear cultural, community, or family systems of accountability?
Two sets of factors tend to motivate change. The first set of factors includes *care*, *love*, and *concern*, which are strong positive motivations for change. The second set of factors includes *consequences* and *accountability*. The effectiveness of counselors, for example, is often determined by how well they integrate care and concern with

consequences and accountability. Consistent application is the glue that holds both sets of factors together.

In the United States, a patchwork system of accountability exists for chemical use and abuse. The trend appears to be improving as evidenced by tougher DWI laws, drug enforcement, and stiff penalties for drug possession and sales. But lack of consistency presents major problems in minority communities where the external systems of accountability (police, social workers, and the judicial system) are not fully trusted and where internal systems of accountability (nuclear families, extended families, and civic, neighborhood, and religious groups) are unevenly developed.

As a result of their distrust of the external systems of accountability, many African Americans have asked community leaders to develop internal systems of accountability. For the most part, this has not happened or was ineffective.

Given this fact, the external systems of accountability must be sensitized to the needs of minority communities, and continuous efforts to build up internal systems of accountability need to be tried. The more functional the internal systems of accountability are, the fewer external systems of accountability are needed.

Are there functional tools to cope with stress?

Methods for coping with stress are often culturally determined or influenced. Historically, religion has been a tool for individuals to cope with stress. Work and exercise also play major roles in relieving stress and tension, as do leisure activities such as reading, listening to music, and going to the theater. Family and friends play key roles in helping individuals get through difficult times. And last, our diet is perhaps the most overlooked influence on our emotional life.

Development of functional methods to cope with stress is necessary if individuals are to reach emotional maturity. Teenagers, for example, are often encouraged to participate in sports. There they have a socially acceptable outlet for their aggressions while learning the concepts of teamwork and good sportsmanship. But when African American youths see drug dealers, gang members, and drug users in their inner-city communities, these youths often learn to use or sell drugs to cope with their problems. When young people are not socialized to look to family, church, sports, or other healthy ways to cope with their stress, two things happen: they become more susceptible to using drugs as a coping mechanism, and their use of drugs further retards development of positive coping mechanisms.

Are there functional rites of passage?

Rites of passage are acts that indicate the progression from childhood to adulthood. Graduating from high school or college, getting a driver's license, getting married, or serving in the military are all examples of rites of passage that exist in many cultures.

When a culture rejects these rites of passage, others generally emerge to fill the void. Many rites of passage that have emerged—participation in crime, teenage sex and pregnancy, chemical use—are dysfunctional both to the individual and to society.

- *Participation in crime.* The extent to which young African American individuals can successfully commit criminal acts often serves as a rite of passage and increases status in the peer group. All too often, crime becomes a win-win situation to young African Americans. If an adolescent boy commits a crime without being arrested, he is viewed as having courage, intelligence, leadership ability, and tenacity. If he gets busted and "does his time well" (without becoming an informant), his stature also increases.
- *Teenage sex and pregnancy.* Many African American teenage girls first engage in sex and then become pregnant in order to

"prove" they are adults. After interviewing African American teenage parents in Washington, D.C., Leon Dash reported that most young girls initially told him the pregnancy was an accident. By the time he completed his second or third interview with each respondent, all of them admitted it was no accident at all. Instead, the girls said that they had hoped to get pregnant, that it is often a way to gain status and attention.[5]

• *Chemical use.* Teenagers often brag about how many chemicals they can consume or who can get the best drugs. It is similar to the game of chicken played in the 1950s, when two speeding cars raced toward a cliff to see who would put on the brakes first. Kids today are playing emotional chicken with drugs. How close can they get to that emotional cliff with their chemical use and yet not go over the edge?

The interaction of these rites of passage are lethal, as we have seen with the number of babies born suffering with fetal alcohol syndrome or addicted to cocaine.

Alcohol and other drug treatment can also become a rite of passage. Adolescents are often showered with accolades for their recovery, paraded in front of community groups and town meetings, and patted on the back for doing the right thing. They recite in vivid detail their exploits while using chemicals and their experiences in treatment. While much of the attention given to recovering teens is appropriate, the process can appear very attractive to the young nonaddicted person who is looking for a way to get attention and prestige.

Many African American adolescents are addicted to a criminal, hustling lifestyle as much as to chemicals. This needs to be addressed in treatment. A positive, yet controversial, aspect of old-style therapeutic communities (as opposed to Twelve Step treatment programs) is that they tend to be more intense, rigorous, and confrontational.

This provides the drama and passion on which many addicts thrive and which may be necessary in habilitative treatment.

THE LINE BETWEEN APPROPRIATE AND INAPPROPRIATE DRUG USE

When the line between appropriate and inappropriate drug use is clear, it stops some individuals from approaching or crossing the line. For example, when there is a no-smoking sign in a room, people generally do not smoke. While establishing a clear line may not prevent chemical dependency, it tends to prevent chemical abuse and, more important, chemical-related problem events for nonaddicted individuals.

As discussed in chapter 1, African Americans tend to access treatment later in the progression of addiction, due to a higher tolerance for emotional pain and a lack of clear cultural norms for acceptable behavior. In addition, the lack of a clear distinction between appropriate and inappropriate drug use in the African American community allows the disease to progress faster and further without significant social sanctions.

The illustration on page 82 shows the importance of establishing clear cultural and family rules around alcohol and drugs.

Historically, groups of people with low rates of addiction have a clear line between appropriate and inappropriate chemical use. This is represented with the first arrow.

The second arrow demonstrates the potential for early intervention. When a culture or family has established norms, it is easier to determine when these rules have been broken and when action is necessary.

Clear rules can be of significant assistance in the treatment process, as illustrated by the third arrow. Adolescents who have a clear understanding of appropriate behavior and expectations will be easier to help than adolescents who don't. The adolescent who smokes marijuana every day before school and sees no problem with that

behavior will be harder to treat than the adolescent who acknowl-
edges that these actions are inappropriate.

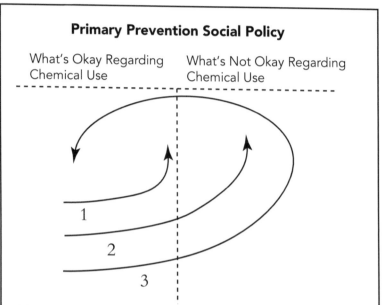

Primary Prevention Social Policy

What's Okay Regarding Chemical Use   What's Not Okay Regarding Chemical Use

(1) This arrow illustrates the preventive benefits of a clear line between appropriate and inappropriate use.

(2) This arrow illustrates the ability to diagnose early when there is a clear line.

(3) This arrow illustrates the enhanced ability to provide successful treatment if an individual knows where the line is.

©2002 by Hazelden Foundation

Figure 11

CHAPTER 7

Issues in Developing Community-Based Alcohol and Drug Abuse Programs

In many communities of color, a wide range of problems and issues exist: crime, housing, health care, education, and employment. These competing issues prevent communities of color from identifying and addressing addiction as a primary problem. In fact, alcohol and other drug abuse can be viewed as a secondary result of other issues. When communities of color do address issues of addiction, they often relate addiction to concerns about crime and rarely go further than looking at the adequacy and availability of treatment services. Furthermore, in this environment, emphasis on alcohol and drug abuse prevention can be minimized.

BARRIERS TO CHEMICAL DEPENDENCY TREATMENT

Some communities and cultural groups are more resistant than others to addressing alcohol and drug problems. Many obstacles prevent these groups from developing alcohol and drug prevention and treatment services. Consequently, professionals need to develop strategies for overcoming these barriers. The barriers include the following:

- protection of community image
- politicization of alcohol and other drug abuse
- normalization of dysfunctional behavior

- impact of integration on community stability
- economic role of drugs
- distrust of mainstream helping systems
- lack of hope

Protection of Community Image

In communities of color, and specifically in the African American community, significant concerns exist regarding how the majority community views minority communities. These concerns present a dilemma for minority leadership. On the one hand, these leaders must own up to the problems in order to deal with them head-on. On the other hand, minority leaders fear that in doing so they will further stigmatize minority individuals and communities. Resolving this dilemma is key to the development of both alcohol and drug prevention and treatment services in communities of color.

Politicization of Alcohol and Other Drug Abuse

Many in the African American community believe that alcohol and drug abuse represents a conspiracy by the majority community to keep African American communities disorganized and powerless. The disproportionate number of liquor stores and bars in minority communities is often presented as an example. In addition, many argue that the criminal justice system has a double standard when it comes to drug enforcement in black communities. This feeling runs very deep and affects the development of and receptivity to alcohol and drug abuse services in communities of color.

Normalization of Dysfunctional Behavior

When a community doesn't have a clear line of demarcation between acceptable and unacceptable behavior, questionable behavior can get accepted and normalized.

The following pattern often takes place. First, there is an effort by many in the community to explain questionable or dysfunctional behavior. This often gives way to excusing the dysfunctional behavior, which in turn leads to normalizing and accepting that behavior. In such an environment, alcohol and drug prevention and treatment services have a difficult time being accepted.

Impact of Integration on Community Stability

Whenever a community experiences rapid change due to integration, or a similar type of social adjustment, natural "antibodies" to addiction are weakened. In such a situation, tools to cope with emotional stress often are less effective. The former rules regarding the context in which alcohol and drugs are used may no longer apply. Methods to communicate those rules may be ineffective. This dynamic has affected Native Americans in the United States, and it is also evident today in Eastern Europe.

Economic Role of Drugs

Drugs have a negative economic impact on minority communities, causing individuals to lose jobs or become incarcerated. Paradoxically, drug dealing can also provide some degree of financial support to families and individuals. A young man involved in the drug trade, often for a short period of time, will provide resources to his family. Perhaps most tragic, a dynamic in many minority communities is similar to a dynamic in Latin America: major drug dealers are viewed as patrons of the community because they support various civic and charitable causes. They also capitalize on a type of cultural defiance that disenfranchised communities feel toward the power elite.

Distrust of Mainstream Helping Systems

Too often in communities of color, individuals who have successfully overcome a problem leave their community. Treatment often encourages this with statements like "Stick with the winners" or "Set yourself for success." Many, however, will return to their communities after treatment. The alcohol and drug abuse field needs to create a supportive recovery environment in every community. If the only way an African American can stay sober is to leave his or her community, the prospects for recovery will decline.

The existence of positive role models is perhaps the most important factor in helping troubled individuals and families see the possibility of positive change and take necessary action. Those who successfully work a recovery program—and who return to their communities—can be these role models.

Lack of Hope

Before chemically dependent individuals can change, they must believe two things. The first is that they are worth changing. They must come to believe that they deserve a good job, a caring relationship, and respect of family and friends. The second is that it is possible for them to make positive change.

The chance for long-lasting change is slim for an individual who does not accept these two principles. Unfortunately, a general lack of hope is prevalent in communities of color and is deeply entrenched in African American addicts, alcoholics, and their families. Instilling a sense of hope is the foundation on which successful recovery is built.

GROUPS THAT INTERACT WITH THE AFRICAN AMERICAN COMMUNITY

Aside from addressing the above obstacles to treatment services, recovery efforts must enlist the support of African American leadership and organizations that provide services to the African American community. Agencies and organizations providing non–chemical dependency services need to understand how alcohol and other drug abuse affects African Americans. These groups need to be motivated to work closely and cooperatively with chemical dependency service providers in affected communities.

Three groups are in close contact with African American communities:

- African American churches
- civil rights and related advocacy organizations
- human service organizations

African American Churches

Why don't African American churches do more to address alcohol and other drug problems? This frequently asked question is multifaceted and complex. African American churches are relatively unaccustomed to advocating nonreligious-based solutions to personal and family problems. Traditionally, black churches are somewhat fundamentalist in their religious beliefs and, as a result, often view addiction as a sin rather than a disease. Prayer is seen as the most effective treatment strategy.

Some churches prohibit any use of alcohol or other drugs. This total ban has left much of the African American clergy unaware of basic issues involved in working with chemical dependency. As a result, many members of the clergy feel inadequate in addressing alcohol and drug problems in their congregations. They may know intuitively that if they raise the issue, a significant number of parishioners will come to them seeking counsel for personal and family concerns related to chemical abuse. They know that they may not have the necessary information and training to provide the needed answers and assistance.

Alcohol and other drug abuse agencies should consider cosponsoring special programs with African American churches to educate parishioners about chemical dependency issues. The key here is cosponsorship. Members of the clergy can then raise the issue with the confidence that they have support and referral sources.

Many communities have an African American ministerial alliance, which is a professional association of African American clergy. This alliance might be willing to participate in "Chemical Awareness Sundays," when sermons are given by African American clergy that focus on codependency, children-of-alcoholics issues, and chemical dependency. After the sermon, one or several of the following can take place:

- A workshop on alcohol and other drug abuse is sponsored by a local prevention or treatment agency or mental health clinic.
- The workshop is publicized in African American newspapers and on radio and television.
- The clergyperson gives the name of a chemical dependency counselor and the times when that person is available. Ideally, the counselor would be available once or twice a week for perhaps a month following the announcement. The clergyperson introduces the counselor to the parishioners. The counselor passes out information sheets to the parishioners as they leave the church.
- Local chemical dependency service providers hand out brochures and answer questions at information booths.

This sort of cosponsorship can happen in a variety of ways. For example, black clergy can be asked to participate in the Fourth and Fifth Steps in treatment centers. The clergyperson should select what he or she is most comfortable with.

Civil Rights and Related Advocacy Organizations

Civil rights and African American advocacy organizations have a mixed response to the battle against alcohol and other drug abuse. This is partly due to the financial support many of these organizations receive from liquor and tobacco industries. They are understandably reluctant to criticize their financial supporters.

Many believe that the liquor and tobacco industries are forming alliances with African American and Hispanic civil rights organizations in order to resist ever-increasing scrutiny and regulation. African American communities need to discuss this issue and break the tacit acceptance of the status quo. When African American leaders raise questions about the wisdom or ethics of accepting financial support from industries whose products cause significant health problems for African Americans, a major step forward is taken in the fight against a conspiracy of silence.

Civil rights and African American advocacy organizations often see alcohol and other drug abuse as secondary to their main mission. As with other groups (African American and white), an unspoken problem may be the chemical abuse among key members of many of these organizations. This type of situation can inhibit organizations in the African American community from taking the forceful action necessary to address the devastating and growing problem of chemical dependency.

Raising issues to these organizations is sometimes possible by contacting a board or staff member who is sympathetic to the issue. The initial presentation might include a brief summary of facts about chemical dependency in the African American community and about chemical dependency's relationship to other problems that the organization focuses on. It often helps to emphasize that chemical dependency is a problem based on a high level of denial. This can minimize immediate and vigorous resistance from organization members.

Human Service Organizations

As in most communities, there is a broad array of agencies and organizations that provide services to the African American community: public-housing programs and facilities, recreational programs, daycare programs, services for the developmentally or learning disabled, youth groups, vocational training programs, and crime prevention efforts.

Staff at these agencies cannot be expected to embrace the issue of chemical abuse in the abstract. They respond more readily when they are shown how chemical dependency affects their issues and their organizations. A person who works in housing, for example, will readily understand and be concerned about how chemical abuse relates to housing issues, such as delayed rent checks, increased vacancy rates, graffiti on housing, and lack of proper maintenance within the unit. A person who works in crime prevention will be primarily interested in the impact of chemical abuse on crime. The unique interests of each group create opportunities, rather than obstacles, for addressing alcohol and drug problems.

When asked whether a presentation can be made on drug and alcohol abuse in the African American community, the staff at these agencies may have a wide range of responses:

- They may readily acknowledge the problem and respond positively.
- They may acknowledge the problem in ways that apply only to that agency. They may welcome the presence of outsiders primarily to solve an immediate problem, such as teenagers using drugs in their parking lot or intoxicated individuals hanging around their building.
- They may be resistant to addressing alcohol and drug abuse issues. They may be threatened or overwhelmed with their own

work and be unable or unwilling to make room for other concerns. Or, certain staff members may have personal or family problems that heighten their resistance or denial to chemical abuse issues.

- They may initially welcome you but later sabotage your efforts. This can happen when there is a change in leadership or when chemical abuse problems exist among key staff or board members.

Following are techniques to increase cooperation from human service agencies:

- Always focus your approach on a specific area of responsibility. Don't expect chemical dependency to be a primary issue for the agency. Apply the problem of chemical dependency to what people in these agencies do on the job.
- Assume a problem-solving posture. When the agency is faced with a direct problem, such as teenagers using drugs in the parking lot, focus on that and try to help solve it. Interest in the chemical dependency issue may broaden within the agency once you have helped with a specific issue.
- Identify those at the agency who support you as well as those who don't. When resistance becomes very strong, emphasize that you are there to solve a problem, not create one.
- If sabotage appears to be based on a staff person's own chemical use, you may have to confront him or her directly.

Inform the agency that alcohol and other drug abuse prevention is a community-wide effort; this lets staff members know they aren't being singled out. Remind staff members that consistent policies across agencies and organizations send the clearest message to the community.

Methods to establish a community "bandwagon" approach are often effective. Some examples are giving awards to organizations that have cooperated or putting an advertisement in the newspaper thanking participating agencies. The goal is to make the establishment of alcohol and drug prevention policy the "in" thing to do.

Establishing Goals for Civil Rights and Human Service Organizations

The first goal in contacting both civil rights and human service organizations is to raise awareness of chemical abuse and addiction in the African American community.

The second goal is to encourage these organizations to establish a policy about alcohol and other drug use and abuse. Such a policy would cover chemical use, or being "under the influence," by anyone on the premises, including staff, board members, and clients. It might also prohibit or discourage drinking at agency-sponsored social events.

Once the policy is formulated, these organizations must decide on the consequences of violating that policy. A statement of the policy and the consequences can be posted at all entry points to the building, where it is clearly visible.

Activities such as sponsoring alcohol-free banquets, refusing to give liquor away as door prizes, and hosting alcohol-free happy hours give the broader African American community the positive message that it is possible to socialize without the presence of alcohol.

A third goal is the establishment of employee assistance programs (EAPs) and client assistance programs (CAPs).

Employee assistance programs (EAPs)

Each organization can tailor its program to fit its needs, but each program should include basic information on chemical abuse:

- definition of chemical dependency
- location of chemical dependency services
- impact of chemical dependency on the organization's mission and goals
- explanation of the organization's policy regarding alcohol and other drug abuse, which should include workplace consequences of chemical abuse, such as suspension from activities and mandated drug abuse assessments
- information about aftercare support activities, such as individual and group counseling, Alcoholics Anonymous (AA), Narcotics Anonymous (NA), and family support groups
- information about social competency prevention programs that develop culturally relevant emotional coping skills
- provisions for diagnostic assessments and intervention by trained personnel

Client assistance programs (CAPs)

Client assistance programs are an important way of reaching out to people who might not otherwise get help for their own or a family member's alcohol or drug problem. These programs are established primarily in government-sponsored social welfare agencies. All new clients in such programs would be oriented to the agency's policy regarding a client's use of alcohol or drugs. Part of the orientation would provide clients with written information on alcoholism and other drug abuse, and local resources available for treatment.

Clients who are suspected of having an alcohol or drug problem, based on presenting criteria, are offered assessment and referral services, either in-house or through an agency. Staff then develops a written contract with the client listing the agency's expectations and consequences regarding the client's alcohol or drug problem. Often, hard ethical questions must be answered: Should a woman's children be placed in foster care if she returns to chemical use after treatment? Should an entire family be evicted from public housing due to drug use by one of its members?

When at all possible, the agency should allow for establishment of support groups to assist clients in living an alcohol- and drug-free lifestyle.

NEIGHBORHOOD EFFORTS: DRUG-FREE ZONES

A major problem in addressing alcohol and other drug abuse in poor African American communities and neighborhoods is the sense of pervasive hopelessness. One avenue of attack on this problem is the development of *drug-free zones* in neighborhoods where drug abuse and the selling of illicit drugs is rampant.

Here are some important steps to follow when developing a drug-free zone in a community:

1. Establish a broad-based planning committee with members who have an interest in the community. This committee might include the following:
    - representatives from social service organizations
    - landlords
    - police
    - chemical dependency treatment professionals
    - representatives from recreational facilities
    - representatives from county or city attorney offices
    - school personnel
    - local politicians
    - residents

2. The planning committee selects a small (four- or six-block) area with a public reputation for drug use, drug sales, after-hour houses, or all of the above.

3. The planning committee declares this area to be a drug-free zone and initiates some or all of the following:

    - A literature drop to every household identifying the drug-free zone. This literature can include information on chemical dependency prevention and treatment resources, as well as information on the drug-free zone campaign.
    - Lawn signs and posters identifying the drug-free zone.
    - Requests that the local police department increase car and foot patrols in the targeted area.
    - Requests to landlords that they issue eviction orders for tenants who use and sell drugs or run after-hour houses.
    - Requests to local treatment programs that they waive waiting-list requirements for persons living in the drug-free zone.
    - Requests to local recreational facilities to sponsor field trips or special activities for residents in the drug-free zone.
    - Billboards with the drug-free message in and around the drug-free zone.
    - Efforts to get the local housing authority to vigorously enforce building-code violations in suspected crack houses.
    - Individuals taking pictures of drug transactions. Safety is an issue here, so residents should be made aware of the risks.

Efforts to create a drug-free zone will likely produce some of the following results:

- a greater sense of cohesiveness and pride among neighbors
- increased awareness and visibility in the African American community of problems pertaining to alcohol and other drug abuse
- a sense of empowerment that overwhelming problems like drug abuse can be attacked by breaking them down into smaller, more manageable chunks

- unification of diverse elements (residents, law enforcement officials, school personnel, and so on) for the purpose of eliminating drug use and accompanying criminal behavior
- movement of dealers and drug customers to a different neighborhood, which tends to disrupt the dealers' business and gang activity
- when such movement of drug activity takes place, that neighborhood will have a clear, close-at-hand model for creating a new drug-free zone

Appendixes
Assessment Tools and Questionnaires

Appendix A
Client Assessment Tools

Cultural Adjustment Questionnaire

1. I can function in most racial or ethnic groups, but I don't feel totally accepted in any.

	Seldom			Always
1	2	3	4	5

2. I don't feel I have a community to call my own.

	Seldom			Always
1	2	3	4	5

3. When I was growing up, I would get embarrassed or frustrated by my parents' attitudes or behaviors that were associated with race or ethnicity.

	Seldom			Always
1	2	3	4	5

4. I feel strong resentments toward *other* racial or ethnic groups.

	Seldom			Always
1	2	3	4	5

5. I reject cross-racial or cross-ethnic marriages as being disloyal or a "slap in the face."

	Seldom			Always
1	2	3	4	5

6. I feel members of *other* racial or ethnic groups view me as the "good one."

	Seldom			Always
1	2	3	4	5

7. I feel stereotypes regarding *my* racial or ethnic group are true.

   Seldom   Always
   1   2   3   4   5

8. I think a lot about issues of race or ethnicity.

   Seldom   Always
   1   2   3   4   5

9. I feel the majority community will *never* fully accept my racial or ethnic group.

   Seldom   Always
   1   2   3   4   5

10. I wish the issue of race or ethnicity would simply go away. After all, people are people.

    Seldom   Always
    1   2   3   4   5

11. My family had/has numerous arguments regarding issues of race or ethnicity.

    Seldom   Always
    1   2   3   4   5

12. I get tense when race or ethnicity comes up in a *mixed* group.

    Seldom   Always
    1   2   3   4   5

13. I get tense when race or ethnicity comes up in *my* racial or ethnic group.

    Seldom   Always
    1   2   3   4   5

14. I feel members of my racial or ethnic group have to sell out to be successful in this country.

	Seldom			Always	
	1	2	3	4	5

15. I have clear racial or ethnic boundaries (friendship, humor, music) in my personal and professional life.

	Seldom			Always	
	1	2	3	4	5

16. I feel accepted by my racial or ethnic group.

	Seldom			Always	
	1	2	3	4	5

17. I feel anger when racial or ethnic issues are discussed.

	Seldom			Always	
	1	2	3	4	5

18. I feel misunderstood when talking about racial or ethnic issues.

	Seldom			Always	
	1	2	3	4	5

19. I feel frustrated when talking about racial or ethnic issues.

	Seldom			Always	
	1	2	3	4	5

20. I think I am viewed as uncommitted or disloyal to my racial or ethnic group.

	Seldom			Always	
	1	2	3	4	5

21. I think I am viewed as outspoken on most racial or ethnic issues.

                            Seldom   Always

                                1   2   3   4   5

Counselors can review the questions with follow-up discussion items:

• What specific situations make you feel that way?

• How do those feelings get in your way at work or in your personal life?

• How can you cope better with the feelings that develop in those situations?

• Who in your life have you seen handle that feeling or situation better? What can you learn from them?

• Create an ideal scenario in your mind for what you would say or do in a similar situation.

• Who is a role model for you on handling racial or ethnic issues?

• What do you want to teach your children/family members about handling racial or ethnic issues?

• What are two or three principles you believe are important in handling racial or ethnic issues?

• What single thing gets in your way the most in addressing racial or ethnic issues (anger, hurt, frustration, etc.)?

• If you could paint a perfect picture of race or ethnic relations in your life, what would it look like?

Racial Identity Questionnaire

Please indicate each of your answers by filling in the adjacent box or boxes.

What is your mother's race? (Mark all that apply.)

- ☐ African American or Black
- ☐ American Indian or Native American
- ☐ Asian American or Pacific Islander
- ☐ Hispanic or Latina
- ☐ White or European American
- ☐ I'm not sure

What is your father's race? (Mark all that apply.)

- ☐ African American or Black
- ☐ American Indian or Native American
- ☐ Asian American or Pacific Islander
- ☐ Hispanic or Latino
- ☐ White or European American
- ☐ I'm not sure

Who had the greatest influence on your racial identity?

- ☐ Mother
- ☐ Father
- ☐ Grandparent
- ☐ Aunt or uncle
- ☐ Other relative
- ☐ Other person (specify)

  _____
- ☐ I'm not sure

When you were growing up, did you live in a neighborhood or community where most residents were the same race or ethnicity as you?

- ☐ Yes, all the time
- ☐ Yes, some of the time
- ☐ No

When you were growing up, did you go to schools where most students were the same race or ethnicity as you?

- ☐ Yes, all the time
- ☐ Yes, some of the time
- ☐ No

When you were growing up, how did your family talk about people of different racial or ethnic groups?

- ☐ All groups in positive ways
- ☐ All groups in negative ways
- ☐ Some groups in positive ways, others negative
- ☐ There was little or no talk about racial or ethnic groups

When you were growing up, did your family teach you about the history and traditions of your racial or ethnic group?

- ☐ Yes, a lot
- ☐ Yes, a little
- ☐ No

Do you try to learn more about the history and traditions of your racial or ethnic group?

☐ Yes, often
☐ Yes, sometimes
☐ No

How or when?_____

_____

_____

Do you take pride in your racial or ethnic background?

☐ Yes, often
☐ Yes, sometimes
☐ No

How or when?_____

_____

_____

Do you participate in organizations in which most members are the same race or ethnicity as you?

☐ Yes, often
☐ Yes, sometimes
☐ No

How or when?_____

_____

_____

Do you ever fear that you are seen as not committed to your racial or ethnic group?

☐ Yes, often
☐ Yes, sometimes
☐ No

How or when?_____

_____

_____

Do you seek out close friendships with persons who are members of another race or ethnicity?

☐ Yes, often
☐ Yes, sometimes
☐ No

How or when?_____

_____

_____

How do you feel about members of your race or ethnicity dating or marrying persons of a different race or ethnicity?

☐ I approve
☐ I'm neutral
☐ I disapprove

Would you take a friend or acquaintance of a different race or ethnicity to a religious or social event attended mostly by people of your race or ethnicity?

☐ Yes ☐ No

Do you think people of other racial or ethnic groups have good intentions toward people of your racial or ethnic group?

☐ Yes, most of the time
☐ Yes, some of the time
☐ No

Do you consider your race or ethnicity an important part of your life today?

☐ Yes, often
☐ Yes, sometimes
☐ No

How or when?_____

_____

_____

When you are around people of another race or ethnicity, do you change the way you talk, act, or dress?

- ☐ Yes, often
- ☐ Yes, sometimes
- ☐ No

How or when?_____

_____

_____

When your parents are around people of another race or ethnicity, do they change the way they talk, act, or dress?

- ☐ Yes
- ☐ I don't know
- ☐ No
- ☐ My parents are deceased

When your children are around people of another race or ethnicity, do they change the way they talk, act, or dress?

- ☐ Yes
- ☐ I don't know
- ☐ No
- ☐ I don't have children

Do you think that in order to be successful in this country, minorities must shed much of their racial or ethnic identity?

- ☐ Yes
- ☐ No

Do you think that your life has been affected by your racial or ethnic background?

- ☐ Yes, mostly in positive ways
- ☐ Yes, mostly in negative ways
- ☐ Yes, in both positive and negative ways
- ☐ No

Overall, do you think people make too much of racial or ethnic issues?

- ☐ Yes
- ☐ No

Overall, do you think your racial or ethnic group makes too much of racial or ethnic issues?

- ☐ Yes
- ☐ No

Would race or ethnicity affect your decision as to where to send your children to school?

- ☐ Yes
- ☐ No

Would race or ethnicity affect your decision where to attend church?

- ☐ Yes
- ☐ No

Do you think there is a white standard of beauty in this county?

- ☐ Yes
- ☐ No

Do you think people of other racial or ethnic groups view issues such as crime, unemployment, welfare, education, and poverty differently from most members of your racial or ethnic group?

- ☐ Yes
- ☐ No

Do you think that your race or ethnicity plays a role in any difficulties you are now having?

- ☐ Yes, a big part
- ☐ Yes, a small part
- ☐ No

How or when?_____

_____

_____

Does a person's race or ethnicity affect any of your relationships with the following? (Check all that apply.)

- ☐ Spouse
- ☐ In-laws
- ☐ Boyfriend or girlfriend
- ☐ Close friend
- ☐ Casual friend
- ☐ Neighbor
- ☐ Boss or supervisor
- ☐ Co-worker
- ☐ Business partner
- ☐ Classmate
- ☐ Social club member
- ☐ Sports team member
- ☐ Member of your religious congregation
- ☐ Doctor
- ☐ Alcoholics Anonymous sponsor
- ☐ Member of a support group
- ☐ Counselor or therapist

For which, if any, of the following does the other person's race or ethnicity influence your decision whether to have a relationship with that person?

- ☐ Spouse
- ☐ In-laws
- ☐ Boyfriend or girlfriend
- ☐ Close friend
- ☐ Casual friend
- ☐ Neighbor
- ☐ Boss or supervisor
- ☐ Co-worker
- ☐ Business partner
- ☐ Classmate
- ☐ Social club member
- ☐ Sports team member
- ☐ Member of your religious congregation
- ☐ Doctor
- ☐ Alcoholics Anonymous sponsor
- ☐ Member of a support group
- ☐ Counselor or therapist

Please add any comments regarding how you feel about your racial identity, any experiences that may be important to talk about, or any conflicts you may be experiencing.

_____

_____

_____

_____

_____

_____

_____

_____

Appendix B
Personal Assessment Tools

Importance of Diversity in Relationships

Number each box on a scale according to the following:

1 = the difference is an **insignificant** factor in a relationship
2 = the difference is a **somewhat important** factor in a relationship
3 = the difference is a **very important factor** in a relationship

	Race	Gender	Age	Class	Education Level	Sexual Orientation	Religion	Physical Beauty	Physical or Mental Disability
Marriage Partner									
Friend									
Co-worker/Classmate									
Sports Teammate									
Members of Your Religious Congregation									
Neighbor									
Employer									
Elected Official									
Adoptee									
Alcoholics Anonymous Sponsor									
Counselor/Therapist									
Total									

Working with Diversity
Your Personal Assessment Tool

		Never		Always	
1.	Do you feel society tries to force everyone to accept mainstream values and behavior?	1	2	3	4
2.	Do you feel society emphasizes differences too much?	1	2	3	4
3.	Do you feel any internal pressure to convey to people different from yourself that you have no racial or ethnic biases?	1	2	3	4
4.	Do you feel competent when you think of yourself working with people who are different from you (ethnically, linguistically, racially)?	1	2	3	4
5.	Are you judgmental of the values and lifestyles in some communities?	1	2	3	4
6.	Are you comfortable with interracial dating and marriage for members of your family?	1	2	3	4
7.	Do you take the initiative in dispelling misconceptions, stereotypes, and prejudices with other ethnic or racial groups?	1	2	3	4
8.	Are you ever afraid of being perceived as racist?	1	2	3	4

	Never			Always

9. Should parenting and discipline styles used in different cultures be given equal legitimacy?   1   2   3   4

10. Do you "walk on eggshells" when interacting with people who are a different age, race, or gender?   1   2   3   4

11. Do you ever feel uneasy with or protective of people of color who are in an all-white setting?   1   2   3   4

12. Do you believe that productivity would improve if everyone had similar work styles?   1   2   3   4

13. Do you feel there are certain American traditions and practices to which all cultural groups living in this country should adhere?   1   2   3   4

14. Do you ever let the realities of racism (lack of opportunity, oppression) be an excuse for unacceptable actions by people of color?   1   2   3   4

15. Do you feel a sense of relief when people of color say they have no racial or ethnic issues?   1   2   3   4

16. Do you feel anger or disbelief when people of color say they have no racial or ethnic issues?   1   2   3   4

17. Would you be comfortable with native or traditional dress worn by your racial or ethnic group in a work setting?   1   2   3   4

	Never			Always
18. Do you ever fear you are seen as uncommitted to your racial or ethnic group?	1	2	3	4
19. Do you allow ethnic differences to be used as a rationale for behavior or action?	1	2	3	4
20. Do you seek out close personal relationships with racially or ethnically diverse persons?	1	2	3	4
21. Do you feel other racial or ethnic groups make too much of differences?	1	2	3	4
22. Do you feel adhering to middle-class values (persistence, hard work, delayed gratification, education, honesty) is a prerequisite for a middle-class life?	1	2	3	4
23. On average, do you feel whites have good intentions toward minorities?	1	2	3	4
24. Do you feel assimilation in the "public square" should be the goal of racial minorities?	1	2	3	4
25. Do you feel there is some truth to the notion of reverse discrimination?	1	2	3	4
26. Does an employer have the right to demand that an employee adhere to "mainstream cultural standards" in dress, speech, humor, etc?	1	2	3	4

	Never			Always

27. Is your race or ethnicity a relatively unimportant part of your life?   1   2   3   4

28. Do you feel pressure to act or talk differently when you are in the minority?   1   2   3   4

29. Do you ever try to establish your credibility with people who are different from you by saying, "I was in the service with..."; "One of my best friends is..."; "I used to date somebody named...", etc.?   1   2   3   4

30. Do you feel we should honor and respect the treatment and role other cultures have for women?   1   2   3   4

31. Do you feel it is possible for people of color to be racist?   1   2   3   4

32. Are whites who oppose affirmative action exhibiting a form of racism?   1   2   3   4

33. Do you feel communities of color must solve more of their own problems?   1   2   3   4

34. Is white privilege a reality in the United States?   1   2   3   4

35. Should race be a significant factor in cross-racial adoptions?   1   2   3   4

	Never		Always	
36. Are we becoming a nation of victims?	1	2	3	4

37. Is it important for persons of color to have
a racial identity?   1   2   3   4

38. Is it important for whites to have a racial
identity?   1   2   3   4

39. Do you believe there is a degree of truth
to stereotypes of men and women and
different racial or ethnic groups?   1   2   3   4

40. Should the behavior patterns and lifestyles of
all cultures be given the same degree of
legitimacy and respect?   1   2   3   4

41. Do you feel that racial or ethnic minorities are
allowed by society to exhibit "racial loyalty"
and solidarity more than whites?   1   2   3   4

42. Based on negative past experience, an Asian grocer
watches young black male customers more carefully
than other customers. Is this a rational and
legitimate form of stereotyping?   1   2   3   4

List the two questions that were personally most difficult for you to respond to and the reasons for that difficulty:

Question # _____

Reason:

_____

_____

_____

_____

Question # _____

Reason:

_____

_____

_____

_____

How might the above two issues affect your working with a culturally diverse group?

_____

_____

_____

Responses to Diversity Questionnaire

Using the lists below, select your most common responses.

1. I often feel different because of: (pick two)

Education	_____	Appearance	_____
Race	_____	Age	_____
Gender	_____	Religion	_____
Class	_____	Disability	_____
Culture	_____	Sexual orientation	_____
Size	_____	Other	_____

Examples for your choices: _____

_____

_____

2. When I initially interact with someone, the difference that affects me the most is his or her: (pick two)

Education	_____	Appearance	_____
Race	_____	Age	_____
Gender	_____	Religion	_____
Class	_____	Disability	_____
Culture	_____	Sexual orientation	_____
Size	_____	Other	_____

Examples for your choices: _____

_____

_____

3. I tend to be most sensitive to differences when they are based on: (pick two)

Education	_____	Appearance	_____
Race	_____	Age	_____
Gender	_____	Religion	_____
Class	_____	Disability	_____
Culture	_____	Sexual orientation	_____
Size	_____	Other	_____

Examples for your choices: _____

_____

_____

4. Whenever I have talked about one of my differences, people have tended to: (pick two)

_____ Minimize or ignore my issues

_____ Show bias or insensitivity to my issues

_____ Overrespond to my issues

_____ Tolerate my differences

_____ Value and accept my differences

Examples for your choices: _____

_____

_____

5. The most common feedback I have received from family, friends, and co-workers regarding how I respond to people different from me is that I tend to: (pick two)

____ Acknowledge differences

____ Tolerate differences

____ Minimize or ignore differences

____ Show support and acceptance of differences

____ Ask others to educate me on what makes them different

____ Try to build a bridge to them using similar differences I might have

____ Show bias and insensitivity

Examples for your choices: _____

_____

_____

6. My ideas, feelings, and behaviors about people who are different from me have been influenced by: (pick two)

____ Reading about different people

____ Working with different people

____ Socializing with different people

____ Media portrayal of different people

____ My religious beliefs

____ My family and friends

____ The law

Examples for your choices: _____

_____

_____

7. I am more open to differences when: (pick two)

_____ The "different person" presents his or her differences in a nonthreatening way

_____ I have had experience with "that group"

_____ I think the "different person" can control or change his or her differences

_____ The differences are consistent with my religious beliefs and upbringing

_____ The differences are ones I have or have had

_____ There is peer pressure to accept the differences

_____ I am not threatened or affected by the differences.

Examples for your choices: _____

_____

_____

8. I feel others are open to my differences when: (pick two)

_____ I present them in a nonthreatening way

_____ Others have had experiences with "my group"

_____ Others think I can change or control my differences

_____ The other person has the same religious beliefs and upbringing as me

_____ The other person has similar life experiences to me

_____ Peer pressure from other associates/friends/peers influences them to accept my differences

_____ The law says they have to accept my differences

_____ They feel we share core values and goals

_____ They are not threatened or affected by the differences

Examples for your choices: _____

_____

_____

9. When a person is biased or insensitive to my differences, I tend to: (pick two)

_____ Inform the person how I feel

_____ Confront the person verbally

_____ Ignore the incident or remark

_____ Make a joke of the situation or remark

_____ Leave the situation

_____ Say nothing, but write the person off in my mind

Examples for your choices: _____

_____

_____

10. Pick one of the following groups that are different from you and that you have strong concerns/fear/judgments about:

African American	_____	Disabled	_____
Rich	_____	Muslim	_____
Poor	_____	White	_____
Asian	_____	Born-again Christian	_____
Hispanic	_____	Gay or Lesbian	_____
Native American	_____	Male	_____
Elderly	_____	Female	_____

Now, answer the following questions regarding this group:

A. What are your most significant personal experiences with this group?

_____

_____

B. Do you feel that you share a significant number of attitudes, values, beliefs, and behaviors with this group? Yes _____ No _____

Explain: _____

_____

C. What were you taught in your home about this group? _____

_____

D. How do your friends/family view this group? _____

_____

E. Do you feel members of this group can or should control any or all of these differences? Yes _____ No _____

Explain: _____

_____

F. How does this group present these differences to you and society?

_____

_____

G. How does the media portray this group? _____

_____

H. What legal mandates are there regarding this group, and do you agree with these mandates? _____

_____

Appendix C
School-Climate Assessment Tool

Assessment of Racial Climate at School

School name _____

City _____

State _____

Instructions

This survey asks questions about racial and ethnic groups. To keep things simple, we use the words *race* and *racial* to refer to the following groups:

African American or Black
Native American or American Indian
Asian American (including Southeast Asian) or Pacific Islander
Hispanic or Latino (whether Black or White)
White or European American

Many questions ask about the *general* impressions you have or others have about these groups, even though we understand there are *individual* differences within groups. We also understand that some people are of mixed heritage and consider themselves biracial or multiracial. When we ask about your impressions of a "group," we do not mean to be disrespectful; we are just trying to get your *overall* impression. Please answer the questions as candidly as you can. Thank you for your help.

How important is race to you in choosing to have a relationship with . . .	Not at all	A little	Somewhat	Quite a bit	Extremely
1. ... a best friend?	①	②	③	④	⑤
2. ... a casual friend?	①	②	③	④	⑤
3. ... a classmate?	①	②	③	④	⑤
4. ... a date or boyfriend/girlfriend?	①	②	③	④	⑤
5. ... a member of a sports team?	①	②	③	④	⑤
6. ... a member of a school club or activity?	①	②	③	④	⑤
7. **How important to you is race as a part of your life or identity?**	①	②	③	④	⑤

For the following questions, mark all groups, if any, that apply. Mark "none" if none apply.	African Americans	Native Americans	Asian Americans	Hispanics	Whites	None
8. From which racial groups do you have **close friends at school?**	①	②	③	④	⑤	⑥
9. Which of these racial groups **object to students in their group dating students** from other groups?	①	②	③	④	⑤	⑥
10. Which of these groups **mix easily with** students in **other groups?**	①	②	③	④	⑤	⑥
11. Which of these groups **mix only with** students in the **same group?**	①	②	③	④	⑤	⑥

For the following questions, mark all groups, if any, that apply. Mark "none" if none apply.

	African Americans	Native Americans	Asian Americans	Hispanics	Whites	None
12. Which of these groups gets **preferential treatment** from teachers, counselors, or administrators?	①	②	③	④	⑤	⑥
13. For which of these groups do **teachers** have the **highest** academic expectations?	①	②	③	④	⑤	⑥
14. For which of these groups do **teachers** have the **lowest** academic expectations?	①	②	③	④	⑤	⑥
15. For which of these groups do **parents** have the **highest** academic expectations?	①	②	③	④	⑤	⑥
16. For which of these groups do **parents** have the **lowest** academic expectations?	①	②	③	④	⑤	⑥
17. For which of these groups is there **peer pressure to do well** in school?	①	②	③	④	⑤	⑥
18. For which of these groups is there **peer pressure not to do well** in school?	①	②	③	④	⑤	⑥
19. Which of these groups get the **best grades** in school?	①	②	③	④	⑤	⑥
20. Which of these groups get the **worst grades** in school?	①	②	③	④	⑤	⑥
21. Which of these groups get into the **most trouble at school?**	①	②	③	④	⑤	⑥

For the following questions, mark all groups, if any, that apply. Mark "none" if none apply.	African Americans	Native Americans	Asian Americans	Hispanics	Whites	None
22. Which of these groups get into the **least trouble at school?**	①	②	③	④	⑤	⑥
23. About which of these groups do you hear **negative comments** from students?	①	②	③	④	⑤	⑥
24. Which of these groups are most likely to **make negative comments** about other groups?	①	②	③	④	⑤	⑥
25. Which groups have the reputation of being **smart?**	①	②	③	④	⑤	⑥
26. Which groups have the reputation of being **stupid?**	①	②	③	④	⑤	⑥
27. Which groups have the reputation of being **good at sports?**	①	②	③	④	⑤	⑥
28. Which groups have the reputation of being **hard working?**	①	②	③	④	⑤	⑥
29. Which groups have the reputation of being **lazy?**	①	②	③	④	⑤	⑥
30. Which groups have the reputation of being **dishonest?**	①	②	③	④	⑤	⑥

For the following questions, mark all groups, if any, that apply. Mark "none" if none apply.

	African Americans	Native Americans	Asian Americans	Hispanics	Whites	None
31. Which groups have the reputation of being **troublemakers?**	①	②	③	④	⑤	⑥
32. Which groups have the reputation of being **respectful to others?**	①	②	③	④	⑤	⑥
33. Which groups have the reputation of being **drug users?**	①	②	③	④	⑤	⑥
34. Which groups have the reputation of being **dangerous or violent?**	①	②	③	④	⑤	⑥

	Very Poor	Poor	Okay	Good	Very Good
35. How would you describe the **overall racial climate at your school?**	①	②	③	④	⑤

	Way too little	Somewhat too little	About right	Somewhat too much	Way too much
36. How would you rate the amount of education you get at school related to the **history and traditions** of different racial groups?	①	②	③	④	⑤
37. How would you rate the amount of attention given to **building positive race relations** at school?	①	②	③	④	⑤

In the last month, how often did you do the following:	Never	1 time	2 times	3 times	4 or more times
38. Laugh at a joke or a remark that made fun of another race?	①	②	③	④	⑤
39. Tell a joke or make a remark that made fun of another race?	①	②	③	④	⑤
40. Confront someone for saying something you thought was racist?	①	②	③	④	⑤
41. Join students at a lunchroom table who were all or mostly of a different race?	①	②	③	④	⑤
42. Not say what you thought about a racial issue because you were afraid of being seen as racist or insensitive?	①	②	③	④	⑤
43. Think you were treated with disrespect because of your race?	①	②	③	④	⑤
44. Treat a student with disrespect because of his or her race?	①	②	③	④	⑤
45. Feel afraid when walking by a group of students of a different race?	①	②	③	④	⑤
46. Talk to a student of a different race about issues related to race?	①	②	③	④	⑤

47. What should school officials and teachers do at your school to encourage more positive interaction between students of different races? (Mark all that apply.)

① Nothing

② Assign students permanently to lunch tables so there is a racial mix at each table

③ Assign students to different lunch tables once a week so there is a racial mix at each table

④ Monitor hallways to discourage students from gathering into single-race groups

⑤ Recruit students to participate in school activities that usually do not attract students from all racial groups

⑥ Assign class activities that involve teams of students of different races

⑦ Other (specify) _____

⑧ Other (specify) _____

⑨ Other (specify) _____

48. What should be done to improve race relations at your school? (Mark all that apply.)

① Nothing

② Assemblies

③ Sensitivity training for teachers and other staff

④ Sensitivity training for students

⑤ Student debates

⑥ Articles in school paper

⑦ Racial relations student group

⑧ Other (specify) _____

⑨ Other (specify) _____

⑩ Other (specify) _____

Please provide the following information to help us understand your answers.

49. What gender are you?
 ① Female
 ② Male

50. How do you describe yourself? (Mark all that apply.)
 ① African American or Black
 ② Native American or American Indian
 ③ Asian American or Pacific Islander
 ④ Hispanic or Latino/Latina
 ⑤ White or European American
 ⑥ Not sure

51. What is your role at school?
 ① Student
 ② Teacher
 ③ Teacher's aide or student teacher
 ④ Administrator
 ⑤ Support staff
 ⑥ Other (specify) _____

Notes

Chapter 2: Impact of Alcohol and Drug Abuse on the African American Community

1. Robert N. Anderson and Peter B. DeTurk, "United States Life Tables, 1999," *National Vital Statistics Reports* 50, no. 6 (21 March 2002). U.S. Department of Health and Human Services, Centers for Disease Control and Prevention, National Center for Health Statistics, National Vital Statistics System, Division of Vital Statistics.

2. Donna L. Hoyert, Elizabeth Arlas, Betty L. Smith, Sherry L. Murphy, and Kenneth D. Kochanek, "Deaths: Final Data for 1999," *National Vital Statistics Reports* 49, no. 8 (21 September 2001). U.S. Department of Health and Human Services, Centers for Disease Control and Prevention, National Center for Health Statistics, National Vital Statistics System.

3. Allen J. Beck and Paige M. Harrison, "Prisoners in 2000," *Bureau of Justice Statistics Bulletin,* NCJ 188207 (August 2001). U.S. Department of Justice, Office of Justice Programs, Bureau of Justice Statistics.

4. Ibid.

5. Joyce A. Martin, Brady E. Hamilton, Stephanie J. Ventura, Fay Menacker, and Melissa M. Park, "Births: Final Data for 2000," *National Vital Statistics Reports* 50, no. 5 (12 February 2002). U.S. Department of Health and Human Services, Centers for Disease Control and Prevention, National Center for Health Statistics, National Vital Statistics System, Division of Vital Statistics.

6. Ibid.

7. Callie Marie Rennison and Sarah Welchans, "Intimate Partner Violence," *Bureau of Justice Statistics Special Report,* NCJ 178247 (May 2000). U.S. Department of Justice, Office of Justice Programs, Bureau of Justice Statistics.

8. The Henry J. Kaiser Family Foundation, "Poverty Rate by Race/Ethnicity, 1999–2000," *State Health Facts Online.* Available on-line at www.statehealthfacts.kff.org (accessed June 2002).

9. The Henry J. Kaiser Family Foundation, "Median Family Income by Race/Ethnicity, 1998–2000," *State Health Facts Online.* Available on-line at www.statehealthfacts.kff.org (accessed June 2002).

10. U.S. Department of Commerce, U.S. Census Bureau, Racial Statistics Branch, Population Division, "Educational Attainment of the Population 25 Years and Over by Sex, and Race and Hispanic Origin: March 2000," *Current Population Survey* (March 2000).

11. U.S. Department of Commerce, U.S. Census Bureau, Racial Statistics Branch, Population Division, "Tenure by Household Type and Race and Hispanic Origin of the Householder: March 2000," *Current Population Survey* (March 2000).

Chapter 6: Cultural Considerations in Alcohol and Drug Abuse Prevention Services

1. Center for Science in the Public Interest, "Fact Sheet: Beer Consumption and Taxes," *Booze News: Updating Advocates on Alcohol Prevention Policies.* Available on-line at www.cspinet.org/booze/beertax.htm (accessed June 2002).

2. "Age of Drinking Onset Predicts Future Abuse and Dependence." National Institutes of Health news release, 14 January 1998.

3. Center for Science in the Public Interest, "National Poll Shows 'Alcopop' Drinks Lure Teens," *Booze News: Updating Advocates on Alcohol Prevention Policies,* 9 May 2001.

4. Nielsen Media Research, "The African-American Television Audience." Available on-line at www.nielsenmedia.com/ethnicmeasure/african-american/index.html (accessed June 2002).

5. Leon Dash, *When Children Want Children* (New York: William Morrow and Company, 1989).

Index

About the Author

Peter Bell is a Minneapolis, Minnesota, resident who is currently the publisher at the Hazelden Foundation. He is a nationally recognized author and trainer in the areas of chemical dependency treatment and recovery. He is a former member of the Hazelden Foundation board of trustees and has a background in business as former executive vice president of corporate community relations at TCF Financial Corporation.

Bell is well known for his work in the addiction field. He was co-founder of the Institute on Black Chemical Abuse and was its executive director for fifteen years. He has served on the board of directors of numerous organizations including the Alcohol, Drug Abuse and Mental Health Advisory Board and National Black Alcoholism Council. He has served on a commission to the White House Conference on a Drug-Free America and the congressionally created National Commission on Drug-Free Schools. He also has worked as a private consultant for treatment centers, units of government, and schools, regarding alcohol and other drug abuse issues. He is the author of a number of books on chemical dependency and was named the ABC *World News Tonight* "Person of the Week" in 1989 for his pioneering efforts.

Hazelden Publishing and Educational Services is a division of the Hazelden Foundation, a not-for-profit organization. Since 1949, Hazelden has been a leader in promoting the dignity and treatment of people afflicted with the disease of chemical dependency.

The mission of the foundation is to improve the quality of life for individuals, families, and communities by providing a national continuum of information, education, and recovery services that are widely accessible; to advance the field through research and training; and to improve our quality and effectiveness through continuous improvement and innovation.

Stemming from that, the mission of this division is to provide quality information and support to people wherever they may be in their personal journey—from education and early intervention, through treatment and recovery, to personal and spiritual growth.

Although our treatment programs do not necessarily use everything Hazelden publishes, our bibliotherapeutic materials support our mission and the Twelve Step philosophy upon which it is based. We encourage your comments and feedback.

The headquarters of the Hazelden Foundation are in Center City, Minnesota. Additional treatment facilities are located in Chicago, Illinois; New York, New York; Plymouth, Minnesota; St. Paul, Minnesota; and West Palm Beach, Florida. At these sites, we provide a continuum of care for men and women of all ages. Our Plymouth facility is designed specifically for youth and families.

For more information on Hazelden, please call **1-800-257-7800.** Or you may access our World Wide Web site on the Internet at **www.hazelden.org.**